D0868402

Secrets

The Trucking Companies
Don't Want You to Know!

How can I make the big money?
Is truck driving really right for me?
Where should I get my CDL?
Which company should I work for?
Should I drive company, lease or
independent?

Yvonne Wright

LULU.COM

Second Edition

Copyright © 2009 by Yvonne Wright

All rights reserved

Published by Lulu.com in the United States

ISBN 978-0-557-04375-0

Printed in the United States of America

Table of Contents

Introduction

"We've got time to think of the ones we love while the miles roll away."
"The Load-Out" by Jackson Browne

KNOWLEDGE IS POWER.

If you are contemplating getting a Class "A" Commercial Driver's License (CDL), you will be doing yourself a big favor by reading this book first. I am your advocate. I am on your side. Before you ever call a trucking company recruiter, I want you to understand the choices you will need to make during each step in your truck driving career. I want you to contrast the pros and cons of each choice before you decide. I will give you information that will allow you to choose for yourself what is best for you and your family.

Trucking companies and schools paint a very rosy picture of the profession. But there is another side that they don't want you to see until it is too late. I will give you both sides of the story. I will clue you in on the secrets they don't want you to know. Trucking companies don't care about what is best for you. Masters in the art of mind-control, they will brainwash you to do their bidding. It's a power trip where you lose. If you go into trucking without this knowledge, you will be like a lamb before the slaughter. By the time you figure out what is going on, IF you ever figure out what is going on, many years may have passed. During that time you may have suffered damage to your relationships, health, and finances. But all will not have been lost. Your efforts will not have been unappreciated! You will have become the darling of every corporate manipulator whose wallet you have fattened.

The jewels presented here were gleaned entirely from my own experiences. You will NOT find this essential knowledge organized in this way anywhere else. The unique value of this book is in the way it is organized to systematically guide you through each minefield of trucking choices and emerge not just unscathed, but victorious! Armed with the information in this book, you will make each trucking career decision easily and objectively.

First you will learn what choices you will make. Then you will learn how to make each choice. You will take Yvonne's Truck Driving Aptitude Test to determine if truck driving is the right career for you. You will learn how to choose a CDL school and the best company to meet your needs. Along the way you will be given a plethora of valuable tips so that your truck driving journey will be less stressful, more enjoyable, and more successful. Pay close attention to the tips. They will prove to be indispensable if you decide to pursue a career in truck driving. You will learn about pay scales, how your pay is calculated, and how to make the most money possible. You will learn how to develop good relationships with important people in your life. You will learn how to avoid log violations, how to get a good trainer, how to choose whether to drive company, lease, or go independent, whether to go solo or team, GPS systems, weigh stations, CB radios, health insurance, and tons of other essential information that the trucking companies don't want you to know! Have fun! *

*Names of specific companies will not be mentioned in this book. My opinion of different companies is unimportant. If you do decide to drive for a trucking company, this book will teach you how to choose the company that can best meet your own needs and those of your family.

CHAPTER 1
Before You Call

FIRST THINGS FIRST! You are thinking about becoming a truck driver. Why would you want to do that? Maybe you have heard that truck drivers get paid a lot of money just to drive around. All you have to do is go to school for a few weeks and then you will be given your own truck. You'll see the whole country! The company will even pay for the training! Sounds good, doesn't it? But don't make the call yet. There are a lot of factors to consider. Read this book first and organize a game plan.

Perhaps you are thinking about calling up one of the trucking companies because their company sounds so great in their web site. You might be watching their videos and dreaming about being behind the wheel of that big truck. Maybe you see an ad in the paper promising you a lucrative career if you call the number. Or perhaps a snappy ad on the back of a trailer has caught your attention.

Please wait. Don't call just yet. Realize that you are only seeing one side of the story. What you see is a deceptively scintillating picture painted for you by the trucking companies. Before you dial the number, it is imperative that you learn the secrets the trucking companies don't want you to know. You must proceed logically if you don't want to become a helpless pawn of a trucking company.

Do NOT agree to go to CDL School until after you have completely finished reading this book. Don't be hoodwinked. Before you make any decisions, it is extremely important for you to understand what choices you have. If you do not understand what your choices are, you are allowing a trucking company to make your decisions for you. That company's self-interests are often not in your best interests.

Armed with the information in this book, you can avoid becoming an unwitting puppet of a trucking company. Learn how to sidestep being brainwashed into making choices that are only in the company's best interests. Learn how to make decisions based on your own self-interests and those of your family.

When you call that number you see on the trucking website or on the back of a truck, you will be connected with a recruiter. This is a secret the trucking companies don't want you to know. Will she give you the information that will help you make a logical decision that is in your own best interests? No! Do you think that she cares about your personal needs? No! Your recruiter's primary mission in life is to get you to show up at her school as soon as possible.

I say, "She" because recruiters are most often women. Around 90% of truck drivers are men, so it makes sense to have women as recruiters. Most men are easily persuaded by females. Your recruiter has been thoroughly trained to hook you and quickly reel you in.

You must realize that the recruiter gets a hefty commission for each person who shows up at her school. She only gets paid when she makes the sale. She makes the sale when you appear in class on Day One. She has no interest in you or what is right for you. She doesn't even care if you make it to Day Two.

If you do qualify, the recruiter will make it sound like she is doing you a big favor by allowing you to attend training. If the school is not within commuting distance, she will direct you to appear with suitcase and bedding on Monday morning at one of their school locations. She will even have your bus ticket waiting for you at the bus station.

This is a secret the trucking companies don't want you to know. This is the first step in the power trip that the trucking companies exercise over unsuspecting victims. The truth is that you are doing THEM a big favor by attending training at their school.

So before calling a recruiter, let's look at the requirements to drive a truck. If you have any trace of illegal drugs in your system, you will be disqualified. Your blood pressure must be normal. Your vision must be at least 20/30 in each eye (with or without glasses). Your hearing must be good. You must also be free of any physical limitations like the inability to bend over or bend your knees. You must have adequate hand strength. You will be asked what prescription drugs you are taking. For every prescription drug, health condition or recent surgery, you must produce a doctor's note stating that you are OK to drive a truck. If you cannot correct the problem, do not consider driving a truck. You will be wasting your time and money by going to truck driving school.

Different companies have different rules about allowable misdemeanors, felonies, and driving infractions. Most companies will not hire you with a DUI or recent felony (within the last ten years) on your record. The number of companies who would be willing to hire you is directly proportional to the cleanliness of your police and driving record. Don't lie to a recruiter about your criminal and/or driving record. They WILL do a background check and find out everything that is on your record. None of them will hire a liar.

Let's get started with some information that will prove to be essential at each step in your truck driving career. What are the choices you will have to make and in what order should they be made?

CHAPTER 2
The Five Major Choices

(1) FIRST YOU WILL DECIDE whether truck driving is right for you.

You will take Yvonne's Truck Driving Aptitude Test to determine whether truck driving is right for you. You may discover that you are not cut out to drive a truck. If so, you have saved yourself a lot of time and money and potential heartbreak and frustration. You can spend your time looking for a more suitable occupation. If your score on the test is relatively high, then you will want to go ahead and continue to pursue a truck driving career.

(2) Second, you will decide where and when to attend the CDL training.

You must also decide how to pay your tuition. After attending CDL School and passing the CDL written tests at the department of motor vehicles, you will get a CDL learner's permit. Then you will learn how to drive a truck at your school. After passing the driving tests at your school, you will go back to the DMV and get your CDL. Once you have that CDL, if you trained at a company school, that company will immediately want to hire you. Do NOT sign on with that company. You can choose to work for any company who will hire you.

(3) Third, you will choose which company can best meet your needs.

If you attended a company CDL school, then you will decide whether to work for that company or switch. After hiring on with the company that can best meet your needs, you will need to complete three weeks of over-the-road training. Some companies may also require you to complete an additional apprenticeship.

(4) Fourth, you will decide whether to be a company driver, a lease driver, or to drive independently.

This book will present you with different reasons for making each choice so that you can make an informed decision uninfluenced by the company brainwashing.

(5) Fifth, you will decide whether to drive solo or team.

You will learn about the factors you will need to consider for each choice. Then you can make a decision that is in YOUR best interests.

CHAPTER 3
To Drive or Not to Drive?

Bᴇꜰᴏʀᴇ ʏᴏᴜ sᴛᴀʀᴛ ᴛᴏ ᴛᴀʟᴋ ᴛᴏ ʀᴇᴄʀᴜɪᴛᴇʀs, let's think about whether or not truck driving is a good career choice for you. Forget any romantic notions that you may have about being a truck driver. Let's look objectively at the big picture. The following questions were developed from my own experiences driving a truck. These are the basic issues. Rate yourself on each of the following 20 questions on a scale from 0 to 10. If your response is totally negative, score the question with a 0. The most positive possible response is a 10. Giving yourself a 5 would mean that you have no bias, you are just neutral. Circle the number that best describes your attitude toward the question.

Please be brutally honest with yourself. It is OK to put the book aside and ruminate. When you are ready, come back and answer the question. This is your career you are thinking about. If you choose to drive a truck professionally, you will commit a lot of time, energy, and money into your training. This would be time, energy, and money wasted if you later decide trucking is not for you. Let's find out now whether you are cut out to be a truck driver.

Yvonne's Truck Driving Aptitude Test

---

1. How comfortable will you feel driving a truck?
Circle your answer: 0   1   2   3   4   5   6   7   8   9   10

PROS: The newer trucks are really quite comfortable. The seats ride on a cushion of air, absorbing the road shock. You can adjust the lower, middle, and upper back, as well as tilt the seat to the right angle. The seat adjusts higher and lower so that you can comfortably reach the accelerator. If you are a company driver and you don't like your seat, the company will give you a new one that fits you better. You can adjust many vents so that the air conditioning or heat hits you just right. The stereo systems are also quite nice with a good range of bass and treble and front and back speakers.

CONS: On the other hand, it may not seem comfortable if you have aches and pains that worsen with driving. If you have musculoskeletal problems, no matter how comfortable the truck may seem at first, your pain may worsen from extended hours sitting behind the wheel. I see many drivers with back pain. They creak out of their trucks and hobble in a bent-over fashion into the truck stop store. I ask them why they continue driving. They answer that they have no other marketable skills. Their choice to drive a truck has made the truck into their painful prison.

---

2. How well will you handle the paperwork?

Circle your answer: 0   1   2   3   4   5   6   7   8   9   10

You must keep up with a lot of paperwork. In order to get paid, you must submit a "trip-pack" for each load assignment. You must fill out an envelope showing every road you took on the route, containing any receipts for scales, tolls, lumpers (guys who unload the truck for you), and so forth. You must also enclose your logs. You must keep your logs current every time you stop for anything. This is quite a chore in and of itself. Many drivers lose their jobs because they have never mastered the art of the driver's log. Guard the bills with your life. The most important paperwork in the trip-pack is the signed bills. If you lose them, you will not be paid. If you hate paperwork, trucking will be challenging for you.

3. How much will you like living in a truck?

Circle your answer: 0   1   2   3   4   5   6   7   8   9   10

PROS: If you choose to drive the long-haul, your truck will be your home away from home. For many drivers, their truck IS their permanent home. Many drivers have TV, DVD, XM satellite radio, internet, microwave, refrigerator, and a small library. Books on CD's are popular among drivers. I have many books recorded on my IPOD, which I plug into my radio. I can hit a play-list and the whole book plays without the distraction of changing CD's.

Some companies have installed bunk heaters under the bottom bunk that can heat the truck in cold weather without the necessity of idling. Many truck stops offer an option of hooking up to a station where your truck is kept at a comfortable temperature without the need to idle, as well as giving you power, cable TV, and internet connections. Your company may reimburse you for this small pleasure. If you don't have your own internet connection through your cell phone company, you can pay a daily or monthly fee to use the wireless network at certain truck stops.

CONS: You may get sick of living in the confined quarters of your cab. If you drive as a team, the space seems really tight. Living a normal life in a home is now an unattainable fantasy. The worst part is not having your own bathroom. This seems to be worse for women. Truck stop restrooms are often far from where you have parked. There may be a long, cold, rainy distance to get to the restrooms. When all of the truck stops and rest areas are full, you can't even park to use the restrooms. I won't elaborate. You get the picture.

If you get a local route or a dedicated route where you come home every night, living in your truck won't be an issue. But these routes typically pay quite a bit less than driving the long haul. New drivers may have a hard time finding a local route. As a long-haul driver, how much will you like living in a truck? Will it be a blessing or a curse?

4. How independent are you?

Circle your answer: 0 1 2 3 4 5 6 7 8 9 10

PROS: If you are an independent sort, you will probably like driving a truck. You are the one who is responsible for getting your load delivered on time. You do not have a boss breathing down your neck all the time, telling you how to do your job. You have a lot of choices and you can make your own decisions about how to take care of business.

CONS: On the other hand, you may have trouble making decisions for yourself all the time. If you can't make snap decisions, and prefer guidance and advice on a regular basis, you may not like driving a truck.

5. How will you do with hyper-awareness?

Circle your answer: 0 1 2 3 4 5 6 7 8 9 10

Your brain must start firing on all cylinders. From Day One of learning to drive a truck until the day you quit or retire, you will need to focus like never before. First you must learn about all the mechanisms on the tractor and trailer and how to operate them safely. You will be responsible for inspecting the truck at least twice a day and all eighteen tires three times a day. You must be hyper-aware of road conditions, your exact location, and what the vehicles around you are doing. Your attention must also be focused much farther down the road than that of the other vehicles. Your stopping distance is much farther now and you must constantly maintain a lot of space in front of the truck, even as cars dart in front of you.

PROS: By exercising your brain, you can prevent your thinking from getting sloppy and slow, and your memory may improve, even as you reach advancing age.

CONS: On the other hand, this kind of stress may affect you adversely. Perhaps you would like a job where you can relax more.

6. Will you welcome challenges?

Circle your answer: 0 1 2 3 4 5 6 7 8 9 10

PROS: Your life will take on a new level of excitement. Each and every day will present new challenges. If you are driving over-the road, getting each new load assignment is kind of like opening up a Christmas present. You might be going somewhere outrageously fun and beautiful. You might get an assignment that is challenging in a good way. Perhaps you will be going somewhere new.

CONS: On the other hand, you may have to drive a really boring or nasty route. There may be wind, snow, ice, rain, traffic jams and road construction. A deer may jump out in front of you. You may hit a cow in the dark. You just never know. The continual challenges may be too stressful for you. Perhaps you would prefer a job with more predictability. How well do you cope with the unexpected?

7. How emotionally volatile are you?

Circle your answer: 0 1 2 3 4 5 6 7 8 9 10

PROS: If nothing really bothers you, then consider a career in truck driving.

CONS: If you are easily angered, you will not last very long as a truck driver. When other motorists see a truck, they think to themselves, "Must get around!" They will do whatever they can do to get around you. They will drive over medians, curbs, into your blind spot, or whatever. They will jump right in front of you, oblivious to the fact that you cannot stop if they suddenly stop. If you become angry, you become a danger to yourself and the other motorists. Do you have the emotional maturity to smile and wave when someone gives you the finger? Can you calmly slow to a crawl when you are tailgated in order to get a tailgater to pass? If not, don't bother to pursue a career in truck driving.

8. How much will you enjoy driving a big truck?

Circle your answer: 0 1 2 3 4 5 6 7 8 9 10

PROS: Many people think it is fun to drive a big truck. They like shifting the gears and the feeling of manipulating a large vehicle around. These skills are very difficult to master. It takes many months of practice to get really proficient. You may feel a certain satisfaction in backing into a dock easily and feeling the trailer pop into the dock. It is a feeling of accomplishment gained after a lot of practice.

CONS: For others, however, driving a truck is just another job. Perhaps they enjoy it at first. But as time goes on, they feel little or no enjoyment from shifting, backing, and manipulating a large vehicle.

9. How will your relationships fare?

Circle your answer: 0 1 2 3 4 5 6 7 8 9 10

PROS: Perhaps you are single and carefree. If you don't have a close relationship, then you don't have to worry about it.....yet. As a long-haul driver, it may be difficult to form a relationship, so you very well may remain single. Maybe it will be good for you to be away a lot. Perhaps you don't want to spend much time at home. I talked to a guy who hates to be around his big brood of screaming kids. If you are like him, you would love to go on the long haul.

CONS: Many drivers are divorced. Many have divorced several times. It is crucial to agree with your significant other about how much time you would like to spend together. One to three days every three weeks is the average home time of a long-haul driver. When you're not driving, you're not making money. If you do get a truck driving job that allows you to spend more time at home, you will be paid less. Give it a lot of consideration. It may be difficult to find a company that will give you the home time you need. Can you find a way to make truck driving work so that you can spend the time you need with your partner and still make enough money?

10. Can you tolerate getting dirty?

Circle your answer: 0 1 2 3 4 5 6 7 8 9 10

PROS: All you need to wear are comfortable, clean clothes. Blue jeans are fine. Do you hate to dress up? No problem. All the company cares about is that you look clean and presentable at the shipper and receiver.

CONS: But if you hate to get dirty, truck driving is not for you. You WILL get greasy and muddy. You will get under the hood and check the fluids. You may get 5th wheel grease on your arms when you couple and un-couple the trailer. You will have to crawl under the wheels to chain and un-chain in the winter. Diesel fuel may spill on your shoes.

11. Will you enjoy driving ten hours a day?

Circle your answer: 0 1 2 3 4 5 6 7 8 9 10

You can legally drive up to seventy hours per week and eleven hours per day without a log violation. With "creative" logging some drivers cover even more miles in order to make more money. Let's look at how much you would be paid if you drive all of the legal seventy hours a week. You will probably drive around 500 miles a day. On the average, it will take you ten hours to drive these 500 miles. Your company may expect you to drive these 500 miles a day seven days a week. That is your legal seventy hours a week.

This is a secret the trucking companies don't want you to know. If your company doesn't pay actual miles (which mine didn't and most don't) your "paid miles" will probably be about 400 miles a day. Paid miles are similar to the number of miles it would take a crow to fly there. You say you're not a crow? Tell it to your company.

As a new solo company driver, if you are paid 23 cents a mile (what my company paid me), your weekly earnings would be $644 (400 paid miles X 7 days X $.23 per mile). Let's say they take out about $100 for health insurance and $100 in taxes and unemployment insurance. Your paycheck would be about $444 a week. That's $444 for 70 hours a week. You would be making $6.34 an hour after deductions. As a best case scenario, let's say you worked for a company that paid 30 cents a mile to new company solo drivers. That would be $840 (400 miles X 7 days X $.30 per mile). Subtracting $200 in deductions would bring your actual paycheck down to $640. $640 divided by 70 hours would amount to $9.14 an hour. That is a bit better.

The bottom line is that you will have to spend a LOT of time driving if you want to make enough money to survive. You won't be paid for days off until you have been working long enough to earn vacation time. A few companies will give you a few paid holidays. But most days you will be driving long hours.

How happy would you be driving about 10 hours a day, day after day, month after month, year after year? How long will you last? If all you want to do is drive, drive, drive, give yourself a 10.

12. How will you deal with good times AND bad?

Circle your answer: 0 1 2 3 4 5 6 7 8 9 10

PROS: There may be lots of times when you will feel great driving the truck. You are "in the zone." Everything is going well. The weather is fine. The scenery is beautiful. Your music is great. The clouds filter the sun into sunbeams that shimmer brilliantly off the line of trucks coming over the mountain pass in the distance. You watch an endless variety of stunning sunrises and sunsets. You are witness to the moon as it goes through each of its phases. Shooting stars scream to the earth. The deer and the antelope play in the fields as you pass. The seasons pass endlessly before you. You are just cruising down the highway and really enjoying your life as a truck driver. At times like this, you just can't imagine why you didn't start truck driving years ago. It's kind of like a "Zen" thing, you know?

CONS: Then there are the times when it is late at night and you are tired and you have to keep driving to get the load delivered on time. Or you are sick and you have to keep driving. Or the weather is terrible and you have to keep driving. Or the traffic is horrible. Or all the truck stops are full and you are exhausted. Or you are so lonely you could cry.

13. How well will you deal with deadlines?

Circle your answer: 0 1 2 3 4 5 6 7 8 9 10

Trying to get your load delivered on time is often difficult, if not impossible. If you don't get it there on time, even if it is not your fault, your driver manager (DM) will not get paid. When your DM doesn't get paid, he becomes very unhappy. When your DM is unhappy with you, you will not be given good loads anymore. He may strand you somewhere with no load out. So getting behind schedule causes great stress for the driver and may motivate the driver to drive in an unsafe manner, causing accidents. When you are not way ahead of schedule, you will receive phone calls and Qualcomm (a communication device) messages from many people in your company asking for an estimated time of arrival (ETA) and reasons why you aren't there yet. You are told not to talk on your cell phone or Qualcomm while you are driving, yet you are expected to answer these calls and messages and still get there without slowing down for any reason.

The only way to avoid this double-bind is to stay way ahead of schedule. Usually, you have plenty of time and the deadline won't be an issue if you don't dawdle. But, if you are given a load that has a very short time in which it must be delivered, you are just going to have to tolerate this situation. Even when you have plenty of time at first, sometimes circumstances just work against you and you end up pressured for time.

PROS: If you are laid-back, deadlines may not affect you. Can you work easily under difficult deadlines?

CONS: If you can't stand deadlines, forget truck driving.

14. How well will you tolerate double standards?
Circle your answer: 0   1   2   3   4   5   6   7   8   9   10

This is a secret the trucking companies don't want you to know. As a truck driver you are often faced with double standards between how you are told to do things and what is actually expected of you to get the job done. You are told not to talk on your cell phone or use your Qualcomm while driving. Yet company members often call and send you Qualcomm messages while you are driving to find out if you are on time or why you aren't. If you pull into a truck stop, you would lose a lot of time and really slow down the delivery of the load that they are trying to get you to deliver faster. I just turn my phone off and don't answer the Qualcomm. I really don't care to be badgered. If anybody in the company wants to know where I am, all they have to do is check on the internet. There is a GPS on the back of the cab of every truck that shows everyone where each truck is at the moment. So why are they bugging you?

This is a secret the trucking companies don't want you to know. It's a power trip. By ignoring them, you are giving them a message that you won't be bullied. Just Qualcomm them when you get to your destination. The same goes for logs. You are expected to be 100% accurate. You are told to log exactly what you do.

This is a secret the trucking companies don't want you to know. But at the same time the unspoken directive is to do "creative" logging. By driving more miles than you could if you logged your hours accurately, you will make more money for yourself and for the company. There are special logging classes to teach you how far you can go with your "creativity" without getting a violation.

This is a secret the trucking companies don't want you to know. Some drivers tear up their accurate logs at the end of the day. Then they make a new log showing that they drove fewer hours than they actually drove. They make sure that the torn up logs immediately go into a dumpster someplace and not in the trash in the truck. If the truck were searched and those torn up logs were discovered, these drivers would be sent to jail for quite some time. These drivers make a lot more money than they could if their logs were accurate. I never do this. It is illegal.

PROS: This is a secret the trucking companies don't want you to know. It is quite simple to avoid log violations and still drive the most miles legally possible. I concentrate on doing two things that I will share with you later.

CONS: If you have a problem with the discrepancy between how they tell you to do your job (accurate logging) and how they expect you to do it (creative logging), you may want to consider another line of work. Can you tolerate the double standard?

15. Can you wait to make good money?

Circle your answer: 0   1   2   3   4   5   6   7   8   9   10

PROS: You must have six months of experience before you will be eligible to become a trainer. A trainer can make almost twice as much money as a non-trainer. A trainer gets paid at his own pay rate for all the miles he drives AND all the miles his student drives less a small weekly payment to his student. When you have a year's experience, if you have your endorsements, you will be eligible for higher paying trucking jobs like driving tanker, doubles, and triples. If you can wait for a while, yes it is possible to make good money.

CONS: This is a secret the trucking companies don't want you to know. You won't make that much money at first. First, you will have to come up with you tuition or else finance it. Then there will be a period of time without pay while you prepare for your CDL. You will get paid a small amount to go out on the road with a trainer. Then there may be more short periods of no pay and reduced pay. When you get your own truck, your pay rate is very low to start.

This is a secret the trucking companies don't want you to know. The odds are that you will not drive a truck long enough to even make enough money to pay for your CDL school tuition! After paying the tuition, many people drop out of school before getting their CDL for one reason or another. They fail a drug test. They can't pass a written test. They can't pass a driving test. Or they decide it's just not worth the trouble. Others just can't make it through three weeks with a trainer. They give up and quit. Or after a week with one trainer, they try again with a new trainer. They may not get along with the second trainer, and try again with a third, or even with a fourth trainer. Or they find that they can't drive at night, or in a downpour. Perhaps city traffic jams are too much for their nerves. They can't sleep in a moving truck. Maybe they don't have the stamina to drive 500 or 600 miles a day. They just give up.

Maybe they do make it through the training and actually get their own truck and drive for a month or two. **This is a secret the trucking companies don't want you to know.** They find that their driver manager (DM) is not giving them loads that pay very much. They may get a few paychecks of $300 a week or even less. They become disenchanted with living in a truck without a bathroom, staying in strange places where they don't know anybody. At some point, the light dawns and they realize that it is HARD to drive a truck day in and day out. So they turn in their truck and go on to something else. Some people get too many log violations and are fired.

There are a few who DO cope with all these hurdles and manage to get by until they are making more money. Company drivers will be able to earn about $.04 a mile more with six months experience. With a year's experience you get another $.03 a mile. How willing are you to wait for about six months before you start making $1000 a week or more as a trainer? Can you wait for a year until you have the experience required to get a higher-paying trucking job? Will you be one of the very few who keep driving until you are making good money driving a truck?

16. How self-disciplined are you?

Circle your answer: 0   1   2   3   4   5   6   7   8   9   10

It is easy to neglect your health. It may be difficult for you to eat well. It takes a lot of discipline to avoid the pitfalls of eating at fast-food restaurants at the truck stops. This may be especially hard for you, because you can get free meals using your rewards points awarded to you when you buy fuel for your truck. Will YOU get fat and fatter? I watch fellow drivers get fat and fatter the longer they drive. Their weight problems can be attributed to the inactivity caused by long periods of sitting behind the wheel as well as by the intake of high-fat, high calorie, low nutrition food. The lack of nutrients in this "foodless food" causes them to stay hungry as their body becomes starved for protein, vitamins, and minerals. If you want to consume a satisfying and healthy diet, you will have to make a special effort to prepare nutritious meals for yourself in your truck. In order to do this, I park my truck at Wal-Mart because most Wal-Marts allow trucks to park in their lot. Then I stock my truck with fruits and vegetables and fish. To cut down on consuming harmful chemical sprays, I avoid buying fruit that cannot be peeled. I do not buy processed food of any kind. I snack on the fruits, and make salads. I make stews in my little 100-watt crock-pot that is plugged into a cigarette lighter power inverter that can handle up to 300 watts total and does not need to be connected to a battery. Sitting for extended periods of time has its own set of hazards. Your body needs a certain amount of activity to stay healthy. Truck drivers really need to make an effort to take time out from driving to get some exercise. That is not easy when you're trying to make a deadline. Stop at rest areas and walk or jog around them. I met a driver who carries a pedometer and makes sure to walk three miles every day. Take your bike and ride on it often. Do exercises in the grass at rest areas or in driver's lounges at shippers. When the weather is bad, do some exercises in the small shower rooms at the truck stops. Don't make excuses for eating poorly and not exercising. Otherwise you will join the crowd of obese truck drivers. How much self-discipline do you have to maintain your health while living in a truck?

17. How easy will it be to find your way?

Circle your answer: 0   1   2   3   4   5   6   7   8   9   10

PROS: If you are like me, and have no idea where you are at any time, your spatial handicap need not deter you from driving a truck. You can get a GPS to avoid getting lost. Even if you are good with maps, having a GPS is a good idea. You don't have to rustle with maps while you are driving. You can plan your route into your GPS before embarking.

CONS: If you are directionally challenged, you may be intimidated about finding your way to new places all the time. Maps may be challenging and dangerous to follow when you are trying to drive at the same time. Some people are intimidated by computers and GPS's. Some may be afraid that the GPS will lead them into a low bridge or a tunnel. When you take the wrong turn, or miss your turn in a truck, it is much more serious than it is in a smaller vehicle. Then you have to figure out how to get back on track without getting on a dead end or a narrow street or a street with low tree branches. You can't do a U-turn. That is usually quite dangerous. How easily can you find your way either with a map or a GPS? Will you be able to find your way in many strange and different places?

18. How patient are you?

Circle your answer: 0   1   2   3   4   5   6   7   8   9   10

PROS: If you don't mind waiting, you will be able to handle truck driving.

CONS: If you do not have patience, truck-driving will be a difficult experience for you. You will constantly run into situations that require a lot of patience. You will have to wait for a long time for your paychecks to become larger. At the shippers and receivers, you may be asked to wait for seemingly interminable amounts of time while they put you in a line to wait to be docked, wait for them to get a load ready, wait to be loaded, wait to be unloaded, and wait for the right person to get around to preparing a bill or signing a bill. You will have to wait in traffic jams. You will have to wait for the weather to improve. When you need to sleep, you will have to wait until you can find a truck stop or rest area that has an empty slot. You will have to wait for your company to correct errors in your paycheck. You will have to wait for the insurance department to get your insurance straightened out. You will have to wait for a shower to become available at a truck stop. You will have to wait in line for as long as an hour sometimes in order to fuel where your company tells you that you must fuel. (The computer finds the cheapest place. Unfortunately all the truck drivers out there will also be fueling there for the same reason.) You will have to wait for a good place to stop to use the restroom. You will have to wait in lines at weigh stations. You will have to wait for your truck to be inspected. You will have to wait for the repair shop to authorize repairs. If your truck breaks down, you will have to wait for assistance. You will have to wait until your DM decides to let you go home. As a long-haul driver you will receive little to nothing monetarily for all your waiting.

This is a secret the trucking companies don't want you to know. You may get stuck someplace for a while without getting a load that will take you out again. This is happening more frequently as the economy falters. It is more likely at certain times of the year like July, August, January, and February. Freight slows down at these times of the year. And when your wheels aren't turning, you aren't making any money. Your company may try to punish you for late loads, even if they were not your fault, by stranding you someplace for awhile. Your driver manager (DM) does not get his commission if your load is late. He may take it out on you by not giving you another load for a while.

You will have to wait for this, wait for that. Are you patient enough for all this waiting and more?

19. How proud will you be?

Circle your answer: 0   1   2   3   4   5   6   7   8   9   10

PROS: You can be proud of yourself for being part of a network of drivers who deliver the products that keep the country supplied with things that people need. You will be one of a select few individuals with the skills, the temperament, and the motivation to drive a truck day in and day out. Your self-esteem will grow as you master the intricacies of truck driving.

CONS: On the other hand, you may feel that truck drivers do not get the respect that they deserve. Perhaps you feel that driving a truck is not as respectable as another profession that you might consider. Truck drivers may be perceived to be rude and crude.

20. How much do you value employability?

Circle your answer: 0   1   2   3   4   5   6   7   8   9   10

PROS: As a professional truck driver, you will have choices about who to work for and where and when you want to drive. You can choose to be a company driver, a lease driver, or own your own truck. You can drive for a big company, a small company, a medium-sized company, or you can drive as an independent, contracting your own loads. You have more choices available to you than in many professions.

Even in a bad economy, truck drivers are in demand. If you become disenchanted with the company you are working for, there are dozens more who may hire you. After you have 6 months of experience, even more companies will be willing to hire you. After a year or two, most companies will hire you. As long as you maintain a good criminal and driving record, your services will be in demand. Even in a recession, companies will be looking for good drivers.

CONS: Do you have other marketable skills or ways of earning money which could serve as income in a recessionary economy (or a depression)? Have you socked away a tidy nest egg? Is there another unemployment-proof profession that you could enter before your money runs out? If you have another source of possible income, then the job security of trucking may not be so attractive to you.

How did you do on Yvonne's Truck Driving Aptitude Test? Add up your scores. If your score is:

0–100 .... Don't waste your time and money. Look for another line of work.

101–150 .... The jury's not in yet. You should reconsider. Read more and decide.

151–200 ... You have my blessing. You are truck driver material! Go to the next step.

CHAPTER 4
Choose the Best CDL School

IF YOUR SCORE WAS BETWEEN 151 – 200 on Yvonne's Truck Driving Aptitude Test, your next step will be to choose which CDL school to attend.

A. There are many factors to consider before choosing a school. Some questions to ask yourself are:

(1) How soon do you want to start driving?

(2) How much money have you saved up?

(3) Do you want to live at home while in school?

B. The three main categories of CDL schools are:

(1) Community college or vo-tech (5 months, cheaper)

(2) Private (about 4 weeks)

(3) Company schools (2-3 weeks)

A. Questions to ask yourself:

(1) How soon do you want to get out on the road? Do you want to get the training done quickly and get out on the road as soon as possible making money? You can be out on the road with a trainer in as little as two weeks if you train with a company school. Or you can go to a community college or vo-tech school and take a truck driving course in which you attend class for a short amount of time each week over the course of a semester. Private driving schools will get you out on the road in about four weeks.

The fast, "immersion" method is quick and easy. You will learn the material more easily and pass the CDL tests more easily than if you were to drag out the training over a longer period of time. It's sort of like going down to Mexico to learn Spanish. You are forced to learn it quickly by immersion in a culture where only Spanish is spoken. In this case you will learn to drive a truck quickly by total immersion in truck driving. The immersion class of a few weeks takes you out of your old way of thinking and converts you to speaking fluently in the language of trucking, where you eat, sleep, and think about how to safely operate a large tractor-trailer. And you will be driving a truck sooner.

(2) How much money do you have right now? If you have enough money saved up so that you and your family can survive for 2 to 4 weeks unpaid, and can afford to make it through another 3 weeks of over-the-road training at the low pay of $350 a week, then the shorter company or private school 2-4 week program is probably a better option because you will get out on the road making money sooner. If you don't have enough money to make it through until you are getting a decent paycheck, it might be best to take the community college or vo-tech route. Then you can keep working at your present job, while you attend class part of the time. You will sleep in your own bed at night with minimal disruption to your life.

(3) Do you want to live at home while in school? If you would be most comfortable spending your evenings and nights at home in your own bed, you still may able to finish CDL school quickly. There may be either a private truck driving school or a company school near you, where you can attend in the day. Sleeping away from home at a company or private school costs no more. If you don't mind staying in a dorm or motel, the company or private school will lodge you at no cost other than the tuition.

B. Which type of school should I attend?

(1) Why choose community college or vo-tech school? The community college or vo-tech alternative is often slower and cheaper. The advantages to this slower route are that you can sleep in your own bed at night, keep working at your old job, and have more time to study. I took Spanish at a community college and was able to learn the language pretty well. When I do go down to Mexico, I can get by OK. I understand the mechanics of the language better than if I had taken an immersion class because I spent a lot of time between classes studying language structure. But if I had taken the immersion class for a short time in Mexico, I would probably be more fluent. The immersion class would have forced me to learn to communicate without first translating the Spanish words into English and vice-versa. Similarly, I think that a longer five-month community college or vo-tech trucking class may give you the chance to study the mechanics of the truck and its operation better, by giving you more time to study. If you scored in the middle range, 101 – 150, on Yvonne's Truck Driving Aptitude Test, and you are sure that you want to check out truck driving, a longer class is a better option. Five months would give you more time to decide if truck driving is what you really want to do while still keeping your current job. Another bonus is that the tuition at a community college or vo-tech school may be lower than what you would pay at a company or private driving school.

(2) Why choose a private driving school? One advantage is that you will have the opportunity to meet and be interviewed by recruiters from different companies. You will be given more information to consider about who you may want to work for later. You won't be exposed to the bias toward one company as you would in a company school. You can use the time in school to weigh the pros and cons of working for different companies. Private schools usually guarantee that they will help you get a job when you graduate. Are you are sure you want to drive a truck? Do you have enough money saved up to cover the tuition and living expenses for a couple of months? If so, the private driving school may be a better option than the community college. Private truck driving schools have devoted all of their focus to teaching only truck driving. These private schools are very motivated to get you trained well and into a truck as quickly as possible.

(3) Why choose a company school? The main advantage is that they will get you through the training as fast as possible. I got my CDL in 2 weeks by training at a company school. You will meet and have the opportunity to speak with drivers who are working for the company. In this way you will find out what it is really like to work for that company. You will learn a lot about how that company operates, how they treat their employees, what their employees think about the company, etc. Although you don't have to work for the same company who trained you to get your CDL, find out the policies and benefits of the companies who are offering CDL training. You need to start thinking about what is important to you in terms of home time, benefits, routes, and pay. If you already know where you want to work, ask that company what school they recommend. If you have already checked out a company thoroughly and decided that it can meet your employment needs adequately, that would be a good reason to attend their school. You would save time by learning their policies and how to fill out the paperwork while you are in school. If you stay with that company, you won't waste time retraining later.

This is a secret the trucking companies don't want you to know. But even though the company has promised you a job after you finish training in their school, if you have not signed a contract you don't need to stay with that same company who trained you. (Don't sign a contract!) Once you have your CDL, you have your ticket to be hired by many companies. You don't have to continue on with that same company. The company with the school that you find most attractive may not be the company that best meets your individual employment needs. Choose a company school based on cost of tuition, length of program, location, and quality of teaching. If you are sure you want to drive a truck AND have enough money to last for a few months AND are willing to live away from home, the company school may be the best option. This is usually the fastest way to jump start your driving career.

Consider CDL school as a separate choice from which company you will choose to work for. The company who trains you will probably be eager to hire you immediately. My company hired me immediately after I returned from the DMV with my CDL. They didn't want me to have time to think about my options. When you get your CDL, tell your company that you will wait before signing on. Go home and do your research. Once you have your CDL, you are free to choose to work for any company who will hire you.

When a company promises you a job after finishing your CDL in their school, they are making it seem like they are doing you a big favor. **They have a secret that they don't want you to know.** Their secret is that when you go to their school and then hire on with them, they are the ones who win big time. They are getting people to work for them without paying them as much as other companies would pay. They have a constant inflow of potential workers from the school, so they don't care about treating them well. There is always another batch of drivers graduating every week. Companies who have schools may try to cheat you out of getting your benefits. They may give you inferior benefits. They may give you crummy routes with fewer miles and more stops. They will waste your time. They will use you and abuse you in more ways than you can ever imagine.

While you are still in school, these companies with CDL schools are getting your tuition money, registration fees, physical fees, money from the food you are eating in their cafeteria, money from t-shirts, hats, sodas, snacks, laundry, video games, and whatever other money they can squeeze out of you. **This is a secret the trucking companies don't want you to know.** After they have brainwashed you into leasing a truck, they can really milk you dry. As long as you are associated with their company, you will be a captive money-making machine. You will be their slave. They will continue to leech off of you until you are able to free yourself from their mind-control. You will be their victim until the day you finally understand how they are taking advantage of you and quit. This could be days, weeks, months, years, or even for the REST OF YOUR LIFE!

When choosing a company school, don't be in a rush. Take your time. Review many company web sites. Call many companies and don't be afraid to ask lots of questions. Ask them if they require you to sign a contract stating that you must work only for them for some period of time after getting your CDL. If they do, pass on that company school. You better shop around! Just as you would spend a lot of time trying on different pairs of running shoes until you found the best fitting pair that are as comfortable as can be, so should you shop for the right fit between your needs and what each company has to offer you.

This is a secret the trucking companies don't want you to know. Ask your recruiter this question, "Will your company teach me to drive a manual transmission?" If the answer is, "No," this school isn't one worthy of your consideration. I think it is extremely important to learn how to drive a stick. Some companies only drive automatic trucks. If you later decide to change companies, you will be out of luck if you can't drive a manual transmission. Shifting a big tractor is not at all like shifting a smaller truck or car. It is a learned skill. The trucks I drove had fourteen gears. Those gear shifts have a lever that you have to hit to go up to fifth and down to fourth. There is another splitter that takes you up and down between high and low in fifth, sixth, seventh, and eighth gears. Low and reverse are just on the other side of a barrier separating them from first and second. Finding the right gear can be challenging. You can only shift at the exact time when your road speed matches your gear speed. You double clutch. You rev up your engine just before you shift down. When you get this down perfectly, then you can work on floating in and out of gear without the clutch. And when you are pulling a heavy trailer, shifting is entirely different than when you are "bobtailing," (driving the tractor without a trailer). You should train on a manual transmission both in school AND when you go out on the road with your trainer.

Which company school is best for you? If you choose a school away from home, living accommodations are a big consideration. If you don't eat well and sleep well, school will be more difficult. My CDL School had dorm rooms. Eight people shared a room with steel bunk beds and plastic mattresses. My room-mates cackled like insane hens until 4 am every night. The fluorescent lights in my face and the all-night-long uproarious laughter made sleeping extremely challenging. We had no cooking facilities or refrigerator in which to keep our food. Studying in the room was out of the question. It was impossible to even talk on your cell phone over the noise in that dorm room. I used an empty truck on the back lot as my study hall.

Tip: Choose a school that offers you a motel room with a refrigerator and microwave. Tell the recruiter that you want to go to a branch school that can offer you a motel room, not a dorm room. Don't let the recruiter bully you. If the recruiter refuses to give you a choice about which branch you will attend, tell her that you will go to another school where your living accommodations are better. It is YOUR choice, not her's.

My company had schools in four different locations. The main branch was the one with the dorm rooms. The satellite schools offered motel rooms. Compare the living arrangements offered to you by different schools. Also compare the distance that you must travel to get to the school. And, of course, compare the tuitions.

Don't expect to get reimbursed for your tuition. **This is a secret that the trucking companies don't want you to know.** If you are thinking about attending a company school, the company will probably entice you by telling you that they will reimburse your tuition. BEWARE! There is a catch. Very few students actually stay with that same company long enough to qualify for the tuition reimbursement. In most cases, tuition won't be reimbursed for a year or two. Long before the time comes for their tuition to be reimbursed by the company, most people either quit driving a truck or they find a job with a more attractive company where the pay is probably better. Companies who do NOT have schools usually pay better. Once you have four to six months experience, you can be hired on by many more companies and at a much better pay rate than you would be getting if you stayed with the same company that trained you to get your CDL. After you have a year's experience, almost any company will hire you at a much better pay rate. For this reason, most drivers switch to a better-paying company before their tuition is reimbursed. If you stay with the company who trained you, you will pay for the tuition in decreased wages that more than make up for the tuition reimbursement.

So, one way or the other, YOU will pay for your tuition. Community college, private school, company school—you will pay. Compare tuition prices at any schools that interest you. They all have finance programs designed to get more money out of you eventually. Do not choose based on the financing. Ask what the tuition price would be if you pay it all at once. At my school, it was $1000 less than the financed price. If you don't have that much cash, you can charge it on your credit card. Once you are working, you can pay the credit card debt off. Remember, this is REAL money that you will be paying.

Tips for choosing a CDL school:

1. If you are not sure truck driving is for you, go to the longer course at the community college or vo-tech school.

2. If you don't have enough money saved up, go to the longer course at the community college or vo-tech school so that you can keep working at your old job.

3. If you want to sleep at home while you attend school, see if you can find a school near your home, so that you can commute.

4. If you want an opportunity to interview with different companies while in school, go to a private truck driving school.

5. If you want to go through school as fast as possible, go to a company school.

6. If you choose a school away from home:
    a. Choose one that offers you a motel room, not a dorm room.
    b. Choose one as close to home as possible.
    c. Choose the one with the fastest training.

7. Compare tuition costs between the schools and do NOT expect to be reimbursed.

8. Do not choose a company school based on whether or not you would want to work for that company. Choose the school as a separate decision.

9. Don't choose a company school just because they are promising you a job when you finish school. When you have your CDL, MANY companies will hire you.

10. If you already know which company you would like to work for, ask that company which school THEY would recommend.

11. Your primary objective is to get your Class "A" CDL. That's it. Find the school where you can get the CDL with a minimum of disruption to your wallet, your relationships, and your life. Don't be bullied by recruiters. Take your time and choose the best school for you.

CHAPTER 5
My Big Adventure

IN THIS CHAPTER, you will learn about my experiences in truck driving school. One day, I got tired of my life as it was and decided to go to truck driving school. I had recently helped my son decide on his own career in truck driving and helped him choose a CDL school. I needed to get a job with health insurance and was looking for some adventure. The idea of driving a truck seemed strangely compelling. Although I have been described as over-educated and have quite a bit of experience in other fields, truck driving seemed to be a good choice for me at this point in my life. Although you don't make that much money at first, with time you can make a decent living. I did not perceive it to be very demanding physically. Heck, even retired people drive trucks. And you can get benefits.

> **Tip: Before you call, write down your work history for the last five years.** Write down the addresses of each employer and the exact dates of your employment. Write down all dates when you collected unemployment. If you were not working for any period of time, write down the reason. If you were self-employed, copy your business license or income tax records. Again, don't lie! They will check everything thoroughly.

I spoke with a recruiter who informed me that my clean driving and police record was more than adequate for acceptance into their company's truck driving school. I decided to go for it. She told me I could pick up my company-paid bus ticket at the bus station. All new students start on a Monday. I quickly packed and was soon on my way. The next evening at 11:30 p.m., I found myself on a greyhound bus to the main campus compliments of the company. The bus station was disgustingly dirty. I waited in line for several hours. When it was finally time to board, even though I was first in line to begin with, somehow thirty or more people shoved in front of me. I got the worst seat on the bus, in front of the bathroom in a seat that did not recline. I guess I was lucky because I did get on the bus. There were many who did not make it. It was a rough night, because it was impossible to sleep in the uncomfortable seat with the screaming babies and little kids. In retrospect, I discovered I was one of the fortunate ones, because I only had to ride the bus for one day. Others were stuck for several days riding on buses across the whole country.

> **Tip: Forgo the free bus ride and jump on a plane.** This is especially important if the school is very far from your home. It's worth it to pay for a plane ticket in order to arrive at school fresh and rested.

When I arrived the next day, I called the number they had given me to get a ride to the school. After waiting for an hour, a van arrived. Ten of us and our bags were stuffed inside for the ride across town. At the school, I waited for another hour for the poor, over-worked woman at the desk to give me a key. I don't know what I was expecting for accommodations, but it was not what I saw when I entered my room. There were eight steel bunk beds with plastic-covered mattresses, some lockers, and a couple of broken plastic chairs. The room did have a bathroom with a terrible smell emanating from the shower drain. The window did not open. I have never been in jail, but I imagine this is what it is like. After dumping my stuff in my room, I hopped on the little company bus and headed out to get supplies. It was tough to find enough food, because our room had no frig or kitchen. But I was determined not to eat in the school's cafeteria, as I felt that the food was not my kind of food, nor was I going to be held hostage to paying their exorbitant prices. I found that by going to the store at least every other day, I could get enough fruits and vegetables with packs of salmon to survive.

Tip: Prepare nutritious meals for yourself. The school's cafeteria is there for one reason only -- to make money for the company. Don't fall prey to eating there. You can eat more nutritiously and much more inexpensively by buying your own food and preparing it in your room. You will need to eat well to do well in school.

Monday morning, I ate my salad in the dark at 5:30 a.m., so as not to wake my room-mates (they had stopped partying at 4). At least I was considerate of them. I don't know why really, they sure did not reciprocate. I showered in the communal bathroom down the hall because it was clean. Then I went down to the classroom early in order to strategically position myself in the front row of the classroom as close to the door as possible. My priority was to get out the door fast so that I could be first in line at the nurse's office when they told us to get drug tested.

Tip: Get to class a half hour early on the first day and sit by the door. When you are told to go to the nurse's office, make haste to get to the front of the line. Some people end up waiting in line all day and part of the next day.

At 7:00, our instructor arrived. He warned us that this would be the last time that he would not lock the door at 7 sharp. Truck drivers can't be late. I found him to be a very pleasant fellow and could see why he was chosen to be our introductory teacher. He gave us a good first impression of the company. He promptly learned all our names and clued us in on what was to happen in order for us to become truck drivers.

Tip: If your vision is not 20/30 in each eye (with or without glasses), or if you have high blood pressure, or are unable to bend and twist or have poor hand strength, don't bother going to truck-driving school. If there is any doubt in your mind that you will pass the drug test, don't bother going to truck-driving school. The tests are very sensitive.

The first order of business was to collect our registration fees, fees for the physical and drug testing, and to show our drivers' licenses. Now that they had that initial money, it was time to start weeding out people. After the initial drug testing, physical exam, and being interrogated by a guy we affectionately named "Hitler," the number of students left in class had dropped from 80 to 45. I WAS the first person in line to get drug tested. There were about 200 people in line behind me. Some of these people were experienced drivers coming to work at a new company. The physical included a hearing test where the nurse stood behind me and spoke softly. I had to repeat the word. Then I had to pass an eye test. Supposedly I had to see at least 20/30 in each eye. But it was really more like 20/40. I first read a line of letters with both eyes. Then I covered one eye with a hand and read the same line backwards. Then I covered the other eye and read the same line forwards again. Those who failed and did not have glasses that would remedy the problem were sent away to get glasses. Then I had my blood pressure taken. Next a chiropractor made sure I had adequate hand strength by squeezing his fingers. I had to bend down and twist around. After passing everything, he signed my DOT card. In Hitler's office, I was asked to admit to any wrongdoing in any way for the period of my entire life. This included lying, stealing, drinking, and drug use. Anybody who was guilty of doing any of these things recently received a complementary bus ride back home. As I am absolutely perfect in every way, I was allowed to continue with my truck-driving career.

> **Tip: When you go to "the interview," be honest about everything that has ever been on your record because they already know about it anyway.** If it is not on your record, why mention it? Hitler is not your friend. He is there for one reason only: to weed out undesirables. If you want to stay in the game, play it cool and deny any wrongdoing. Deny, deny, deny! He will ask you when the last time was that you ever smoked pot, or took any kind of drugs. If you were never arrested for drugs, the correct answer is NEVER! Drugs are illegal. You should tell him that you do not drink alcohol. Of course, we have all had a drink in the past, perhaps in high school or college. But you wisely do not drink any more. Truck drivers do not drink alcohol! If you do have a recent history of drug use, don't bother going to truck driving school at all. To drive a truck, it is absolutely necessary to be drug and alcohol-free in order to keep our roadways safe.

In the afternoon, I returned to the classroom where we received a little green truck drivers' Bible. We referred to this to answer a test. If you failed this test, you were given another opportunity to take the test. The test was easy if you were fairly literate in the English language. This weeded out another 10 people.

The next two days we studied for the written CDL tests. The instruction was excellent. We were given a CDL manual as well as actual questions and answers that had appeared on CDL tests. Our instructor went over and over the questions until we really knew the answers. We took many practice tests in class to assure our mastery of the material. On Wednesday afternoon a finance company guy came in and made us all sign forms stating that we would be responsible for paying the finance company for our tuition. Despite much complaining, everyone signed the forms. Anyone who did not subsequently pass the written exams given at the department of motor vehicles would still be responsible for paying their tuition of $3000 (if you financed through the company's finance company) plus finance charges and any late fees. You are given more opportunities to take the CDL written tests if you fail. Also some of the drug tests had not been returned. If you failed those drug tests, you would still be responsible for paying the tuition. You don't get any second chances on drug tests.

> **Tip: This is a secret that the trucking companies don't want you to know about.** If you have any doubt about your ability to pass the drug tests or the written CDL tests, do NOT go to truck-driving school.   By signing the finance agreement, you are committing yourself to paying for your tuition even if you fail the drug test or the CDL tests. They can get your tuition money without even training you!

> **Tip: This is another secret the trucking companies don't want you to know.** It is better to pay the credit card interest on a smaller amount, in my case, $1995, than the finance company's interest on a greater amount, in my case, $3000. If you do pay in full, save that receipt and watch your paychecks to make sure that payroll is not deducting tuition payments. Don't count on the company reimbursing your tuition. Most people will never work for that company long enough to meet the reimbursement requirement of a year or more. The tuition is the price you pay for getting that CDL. It would be much more difficult to get one on your own. How would you take the driving test without a truck and without having learned how to drive it?

The next day a few more people were eliminated because their drug tests came back positive. One guy went ballistic, and after his raging was met with a bus ticket home, he went up to his dorm room and stole everything of value from his seven room-mates, including DVD players, IPODS, computers, and money. He sneaked out and was never caught. Speaking of thieves, a woman checked into the dorm late one night and went through everyone's bags as they slept and stole everything she wanted. This story had a happier ending than the one about the disgruntled drug test failure guy. Someone woke up and called security and she was apprehended. She was a homeless woman who was admitted by the front desk, no questions asked.

> **Tip: Keep your valuables on your person at all times.** Wear a money belt with your driver's license, cash, checks, and credit card zipped inside. You can buy one at the army surplus store or a travel store. Tuck the money belt inside your clothes. Don't bring a computer or anything valuable that you don't absolutely need. Bring as little as possible. Keep anything that you think anybody might steal locked in a locker.

First thing Thursday morning we crammed one last time for the written tests and then went down to the DMV. A few people had to go to the Social Security office first, because they did not have an intact Social Security card. If a little corner is ripped off your card, it is no good. These people could not take the written CDL tests until they got a new Social Security card. At the DMV, as I had lost my driver's license and just had a temporary, I was told to come back the next day to test. They needed to check with my home state to make sure I was for real. I returned to school and studied some more and then came back the next day. You had a choice of taking printed or computer CDL tests. I chose the computer. People later told me that the printed tests were easier. That may or may not be true. There were a few tricky questions. If you didn't pass the first time, you had one more chance to take the test over that same day. Several people did not pass, even after the second try. These students started school all over again the next Monday, studying with the new class coming in. Some students repeated this process for several weeks before passing the CDL tests at the DMV.

> **Tip: READ the CDL manual. Get your social security card** before you go to truck driving school. Study the test questions and answers given to you in class until you know them well. Then when you are taking the tests, relax and take the time to read each question carefully. Formulate the answer in your mind before looking at the multiple choices. Then look for that answer in those multiple choices. When in total doubt, choose "c." If you know it's not "c" then choose "b."

> **Tip: If you are dyslexic, you may request to have the tests spoken aloud.** Check with the state where you will be testing. You may have to make this request a week ahead of your test date. Some people find this to be very helpful, as the spoken voice may have a bit of a different inflection when speaking the correct choice.

After passing all three tests at the DMV, it was back to the classroom for more study. We were now ready to get into the truck and learn how to drive it. We learned proper entry and exit, how to couple the tractor onto the trailer via the 5th wheel, and how to crank the landing gear up and down. We learned how to adjust the seats, what the gauges showed and how to inspect the truck.

Friday was our last chance to pay our tuition in full for $1995 instead of $3000 financed. I charged the full $1995 on my credit card and asked for the finance agreement to be shredded. They gave me a receipt showing payment in full.

> **Tip: Don't lose your tuition payment receipt.** The payroll department may later deduct tuition payments from your paychecks, even though you have already paid for your tuition.

> **Tip: When learning to back up the truck, wear a hat, long sleeves and sunscreen if you are fair-skinned and it is summer.** You spend a lot of time in the hot sun spotting while others are backing. You could burn to a crisp out there on the asphalt.

Next we began with the hardest skill of all—backing up. Unfortunately for us, the regular backing instructor had been out partying late on Friday night and called in sick on Saturday. We were stuck with another young "backing instructor" who had no idea how to teach. When we went out on the backing course to learn, there were so many people in our class that it was hard to hear what the instructor told us. He was sitting in the cab with the engine running. He had the window rolled down and was talking to the group out of the window. It was especially tough for me because most of the class was smoking cigarettes. I needed to breathe air, so I was standing away from the smoke. (I would estimate that 90% of truckers smoke.) I didn't hear a word he said. Then we each took turns backing the truck with our instructor inside. When it was my turn to try, he kept screaming at me, "Why are you turning the wheel so much? Why are you turning the wheel the wrong way?" and so forth. I had no idea how to back a truck and did not appreciate his temper tantrum. After he left, some of the guys in the class were nice enough to show me how to back the truck. Sometimes it helps to be female . . . or not. It seems like guys have a natural "feel" for driving that I don't have. Of course, I didn't play with toy trucks when I was a little, either. I practiced backing the rest of the day and felt I was ready to take the test the next morning.

Tip: DON'T test until you are absolutely 100% sure you that you will pass with flying colors! You get only 3 chances to pass the backing test. If you fail the third time, you will go home. This is a fabulous opportunity to practice backing the truck. Take as much time as they will give you to practice. You might not get a chance to practice backing like this again until you get your own truck.

Sunday morning I took the test, but got so nervous that I failed miserably. Our young instructor would shout loudly, "Encroachment!" every time a tire would hit a line. I really got flustered about this. After failing the test, I practiced backing up all day and into the night until I was sure I could pass. Monday morning of the second week took us to a new classroom where we learned the basics of shifting, turning, stopping, and mountain driving. We studied in the classroom for a couple of hours and then split up into groups of two or three and went out with our driving instructors. My new instructor, Tom, was super nice. After I told him about my backing problems, he became very angry with the young backing instructor. This time when I tested with Tom, I aced the backing test.

Learning to shift gears was much harder than I had anticipated. It was especially hard for me because I had driven stick for many, many years and I had to unlearn the habits I had formed. Shifting the big truck is considerably different from shifting other vehicles. You can only shift when your gear speed exactly matches your road speed. Then you double clutch. When shifting down, you must rev the engine up after you take it out of gear. It takes a lot of concentration to shift and still pay attention to keeping the truck centered in your lane. After you have been driving for a while, you may learn to "float" the gears without the clutch. Tuesday and Wednesday, after attending class, we concentrated on learning how to turn. As I still had not mastered shifting, I found it difficult to shift AND turn. The trick to turning is to set up the turn early by keeping your rig wide. Take as much space as you can by going straight forward before you start the turn. Watch your tandems (the double set of wheels at the rear of the trailer) and make sure they are clear before you proceed. You must also remember to cancel your turn signal after turning. The turn signal doesn't cancel itself like in a car.

Tip: Practice shifting an imaginary truck over and over again until you don't have to think where the gears are located and you are revving the engine up every time you downshift. Don't wear boots when you are learning. Wearing tennis shoes will allow you to feel the truck better.

Thursday, we learned how to drive in the mountains. That was an eye-opener because you really have to think ahead about getting your rpms up when climbing a hill before you shift. It is also extremely important to slow your speed and get into a lower gear as you crest the hill. You must learn to control the truck, not let the truck control you. Friday, we were tested on inspections and then were given a road test. As I still was not confident about my shifting, I elected to wait until the following week to road test, so that I could get some more practice shifting.

This is a secret the trucking companies don't want you to know. Beware of being brainwashed to lease a truck. On Saturday and Sunday we were forced to sit through a long presentation about how to successfully run your own business (lease a truck). What the company was really doing was brain-washing the students to lease a truck. I saw this subtle brain-washing from Day One. There are big signs all over the place with slogans like, "Head Honcho, Master of Your Own Destiny" and stuff like that playing up to your ego. They are constantly telling you how your credit doesn't matter, how you can take a pet in your lease truck but not a company truck, and how you can choose the color of the truck.

Tip: Just as in backing, do NOT take the driving test until you are totally confident about your abilities. You are not in competition with your classmates. Some of us need more practice. Again, if you fail three times, you'll get a bus ticket home. It is better to wait and spend more time practicing with your instructor than to take the test and fail. It doesn't cost you a penny more to spend more time practicing. Failing is no fun, and it's tough on your self-esteem.

I spent Monday and Tuesday of the next week practicing driving around town with Tom and finally testing. Tom was really cool because he knew how nervous I get when being tested. So he tested me without telling me that he was testing me. I passed. I was given a sealed envelope with my passing test scores, told not to open it, and sent to the DMV. After going down to the DMV with my paperwork, I was issued my CDL. Immediately upon my return, I was hired by the company. I was thrilled. As my over-the-road trainer would not be there to pick me up for two days, I was paid a token $50 a day (a bribe to make sure that I would not look for a job elsewhere). I had to report to the office in person each morning so that they knew I was still there and not out checking out other trucking companies. I used the time to recover from a nasty cold that was going around the dorm.

I just wish that I knew then what I know now. I wish somebody had written this book for ME to read before I started this whole truck driving adventure. I am glad, however, that I can save you from being used and abused by a trucking company! If I had known all this, I would have taken my CDL and looked for a job with a different company.

This is a secret the trucking companies don't want you to know. We had been told that in order to be hired on by the company, we must immediately start training as soon as we got our CDL. We were NOT allowed to go home. We were brainwashed into thinking we could not leave. From Day One, we were trained to think how great it was going to be to work for this company. What a privilege it would be to drive for this company, the best trucking company in America. Blah, Blah, Blah. And we bought it. Hook, line, and sinker. I never seemed to notice that the company where I trained offered the worst pay scale in the industry. I never questioned anything. I did as I was told. They played me like a violin. They tried to cheat me at every juncture. As time went on they tried to cheat me out of my home time, my benefits, my pay, and my sanity. This cheating did not escape my attention, however. By standing up for my rights, the company's selfish intention was averted. You will understand more about this as I go on.

CHAPTER 6
Choose the Best Company

T HE FIRST THING YOU NEED TO DO before choosing a company is to prioritize your needs. Get a notebook and write down every need you have. Then prioritize them in order of importance to you.

1. What is your most important need? The most important need for me is to be with my husband as much as possible. Since he doesn't want to drive as a team or ride as a passenger in my truck, I want to be home as much as possible. Ideally I would like to be home every night. If that isn't possible, I would want to be home at least 2 days out of each week. I would also accept a job where I could work a week and be home a week. I don't care if I don't get my own truck, as long as I could be home one week out of two. "Slip-seating" means that you don't have a truck that is exclusively for your own use. Instead you use whatever truck is available and then turn it in before you take your break so that someone else can drive it while you are home. But I would not drive a truck that has been driven by anybody who smokes. That would be intolerable. You may not care as much about home time, especially if you are not married.

2. What is your second most important need? I want good health insurance with no pre-existing condition clause and to be able to see any doctor.

3. What is your third most important need? Mine is how much money I can make. To find this out I need to know the paid miles per week driven by the average driver for their company. I can find this out by calling the company. Then I would multiply that by the cents per mile I would be getting. That can be found on the company driver pay scale on their internet site. I would look on the solo scale as I do not want to drive team. Then I would look for the row matching my length of experience to find the cents per mile. Cents per mile times average paid miles per week shows me how much money I would be making.

What other needs do you have? These are mine:

4. I don't like to drive at night.

5. I would like to get a dedicated route with a lot of highway miles. Again I need to find out the average weekly miles on the route to find out the pay.

6. I would look for the highest percentage of drop and hook.

7. I would not work for a company where the trucks must be tarped.

8. I would prefer to work for a company that pays for actual miles driven between destinations instead of miles that the crow flies. I am not a crow.

9. I do not want to drive in hazardous weather conditions.

Now let's look at how different companies may be able to meet those needs. We will examine health insurance, check out the local and long-haul opportunities and learn pertinent questions that must be asked before choosing a company.

A. Health Insurance.

My benefits were supposed to start after ninety days. After I had been employed for sixty days, I double-checked and was assured that everything was in order. After I had been employed for ninety days, I saw no deductions for health insurance on my paycheck. The 401K company did not have any record of me. It was very difficult to get through to the insurance department at my company to find out what was going on. My calls were not returned. After several days and loud complaining to human resources, I finally got through to the insurance department who told me that I had never filled out any paperwork. HMMMMM!!!!!! My health, dental, vision, and 401K paperwork had mysteriously vanished. The insurance department sent me new insurance forms which I filled out again, and then faxed them back AND sent certified mail to prove that they got them. A few months later when my husband needed glasses, I went through the same thing again when they told me that I had not requested vision insurance (even though I most certainly had).

> **Tip: Make a copy of all your benefit forms after you fill them out and keep them somewhere safe. This is another secret that the company doesn't want you to know.** After I was hired, the company "lost" all of my benefit forms. As they must pay for part of your benefits, it is not in their best interests for you to get benefits.

> **Tip: Immediately after being hired, march into the company's insurance office and ask to see all of the paperwork that you have filled out.** Get a letter signed and dated by the insurance department manager stating that your benefits, including 401K, health, dental, and vision insurance will begin without fail on the date that the company has promised you they will begin. Also ask the insurance department for specifics about health insurance coverage for pre-existing conditions and prescription coverage. Get it in writing.

It was my understanding that group insurance was, by law, not allowed to disallow payment for pre-existing conditions. Surprise, surprise, surprise! After my insurance finally kicked in, after all my haggling with the company insurance department, I received a letter from the insurance company stating that they would not cover any conditions that had been in existence six months before my first day of employment until six months after the first day of my insurance coverage! They would not even pay for prescriptions that had been previously prescribed.

Getting the insurance company to pay for coverage you are supposed to get can also be challenging. When my husband needed surgery, I called the insurance company to make sure that they would pay for it. I was told that they routinely deny every claim when it is first submitted. In order to get the insurance company to pay, I would have to keep calling and complaining. This was unacceptable to me. I asked to speak to the supervisor. After much arguing, the supervisor, Lisa, said they would cover it. Then the billing secretary at the doctor's office, Pat, called them and got the same run-around. Pat called me and said that they weren't going to pay. I told her to ask for Lisa. She finally got the OK. He got the surgery two months ago, and still the insurance has only paid a small portion. They want more and more paperwork in order to delay payment. You really have to keep after them to get them to pay.

B. Check out the local opportunities FIRST!

Do you want to be home with your family each night? If so, check out the opportunities for class A CDL drivers in the vicinity of your home. Check around locally first even if you don't mind being away from home.

It is possible (but not probable) that you may find a better-paying job at home than you would at an interstate trucking company. Often local companies will give you benefits that begin on the first day you begin work. The interstate companies make new drivers wait sixty to ninety days to begin getting their benefits.

If you drive locally, you won't have to waste time, energy, and aggravation by training for another three to seven weeks, either. If you get a local job driving a big tow truck, you may do quite well getting commissions when working overtime, especially in the winter in a place where it snows a lot. Garbage companies may also offer a nice paycheck.

Check the want ads in the newspapers. Companies who advertise here are usually desperate for drivers. Check with the local employment office. Look in the phone book for any kind of trucking companies. Do not call them. Make up a resume using a resume template off the internet. Then drive around and make a personal visit to each of them so that they can see your eager, shining face, your resume, and your CDL. Each time you visit a trucking company, make a separate page in your notebook for that company. Write down the date, time, and person's name with whom you spoke. Note whatever they tell you about the job, anything you need to do to get the job, who you should talk to, and when would be a good time to check back with them. Ask them questions concerning their ability to meet your own needs. Would working for this company meet all of your needs? Ask them questions 1 – 14 in section D.

Tip: If you find a local company that interests you, but they tell you they don't need you, don't give up. Repeatedly return. Speak with the manager, not human resources.

You may stumble onto a fantastic opportunity right near your home! If they say they will hire you and it looks like they can adequately meet your needs, the correct answer is, "YES!" Why look further?

C. Then check out long-haul companies.

If you don't find a local job that suits you and if you don't mind being away from home, get on the internet and check out CDL opportunities for drivers whose home is in your state. There are a multitude of internet sites that will be glad to take your information and forward it to trucking companies. Only give them your e-mail address. If you decide to give out your correct phone number, be prepared for a bunch of recruiters to call you on a regular basis for the next ten years or so. If you don't mind changing your phone number soon, go ahead and give out your number.

Do an internet search for "(the name of your state) truck driving jobs." For instance, http://www.bigtruckdrivingjobs.com is a particularly good site because it has every company listed that is hiring drivers from your state. Then systematically go down the list clicking on every company. If you can see right away that you do not qualify to work at that company or that the company will not meet your needs, eliminate it. If it looks like an OK company, write down the company name and phone number on a separate page in your notebook.

In my case the most important thing is home time, then health insurance, and then paid miles per week multiplied by cents per mile. Since I want more home time than most companies are willing to give, I can narrow down my own list just by eliminating those companies that won't give me enough home time. If a company is willing to let you have more home time than once every three weeks, it will probably say so. If home time is not listed and the company looks interesting to me in other ways, I might check their website and call the company. So right there I have narrowed down my list of acceptable companies from sixty-one to four.   Now I have written down the names of four companies.

Next I can consider my second need, insurance. I will check the companies' websites. If I can't find the information I need there, I will call the company and ask to speak with the insurance department.   I will compare the plans of each company and eliminate any that only let you go to certain doctors. I do not want to be told what doctor I can see. Then I will eliminate any with pre-existing condition clauses. Two of the four companies on my list have unacceptable insurance plans.

Now I have narrowed my list of acceptable companies down to two. Now it is easy. What are the average paid miles per week? What is the cents per mile rate that I would be paid? Multiply. Which company would be paying me more money per week? This narrows it down to one. I would then call that company and ask them all of the questions in the next section. I will keep searching for a company that can meet my needs.

Do the same with your own list of companies that meet your needs. If you don't have such strict home time needs, your list will probably be much longer than mine. Call each company that meets your needs and ask them all of the questions in the next section. Carefully note all of their responses in your notebook. Then sit down and take the time to compare the companies based on their responses. The chances are that one company will stand out as best meeting your needs. Give them a call and chat some more. If you think you would like to work for this company, find out how soon you can be trained.

Tip: Ask for the phone number of the training placement coordinator. Call the placement coordinator and request a trainer who is as much like you as possible: a smoker/non-smoker, neat/cluttered, clean/messy, or male/female. If you are female and they won't give you a female trainer, stress the importance of getting a male trainer who will respect your boundaries. Be prepared to wait for this person to become available. It is well worth the wait.

D. What questions should I ask?

1.   Find out exactly WHEN your benefits will kick in after you are hired. If you or a family member ever has medical bills, your insurance coverage will be critical. Then insurance will become much more important than what the company is paying you. If your insurance is nonexistent or poor, you could get yourself into deep debt with just one serious illness or accident. Don't under-play the importance of good health insurance.

2.   How much does the insurance cost per week for me, for my family?

3.   Find out the company names of their insurance plans and if you have the option of seeing any physician that you want to. Download the brochure from the internet.

4.   Does the health insurance cover physical therapy, mental health?

5.   What are the deductibles and co-pays?

6.   What about prescription coverage? Pregnancy? Preventative care?

7.   Does the insurance plan come with a pre-existing condition clause? None is best.

8.   Will I have to drive at night?

9.   What is your average weekly mileage? **This is a secret the trucking companies don't want you to know.** If you spend a lot of time hanging around shippers and receivers, you won't make very much. Who cares if they give you $10 at each receiver when you have wasted hours? How many miles you will drive in an average each week is what matters.

10.   How much would I be paid in cents per mile?

11.   Do you pay actual miles or "Rand-McNally" miles? This is a secret the companies don't want you to know. Ask if those miles are actual miles driven or some other form of miles, calculated to cheat you.

12.   Do you require any endorsements on my CDL? If haz-mat, tanker, and/or doubles and triples endorsements are required, you should expect to get better pay. Usually these jobs only are available to drivers with a year or more experience.

13.   Are your trailers tarped? Tarping is a giant pain. It is hard, hard work and ridiculous in wind. Forget about working for a company whose trailers are tarped.

14.   What kind of truck will I be driving? This is a secret the companies don't want   you to know. Late model, manual transmissions are the best. You want to train on a manual transmission so that you will be a versatile driver. Manual transmissions make it easier to control the rig, especially in the mountains and on ice. If you are driving in southern climes and flat roads, the type of transmission is not such a big deal.

15.   How often will I get home? How often do you want to take home time? Do you want to go home once a week, every day, once every three weeks, or would you rather be out on the road most or all of the time? When you are driving long-haul, you usually get one day off for every three weeks that you drive. However, some companies may offer new drivers more home time with special programs. If you want to go home to be with your family, it is extremely important to find out how often and for how long you will be allowed to go home. And remember also that you will not be paid when you are at home. If home-time is important to you and you want to be home more often than once every three weeks, you will find that your choices have dwindled down considerably right there.

16.   How long can I spend at home? Typically it is one day per week driven.

17.   What dedicated routes are available in my area? **These are secrets the trucking companies don't want you to know.** How many payable miles a day will you get? How much time will you waste at shippers and receivers? How often can you go home? Do the routes end near your home? Or will you have to drive a long way to get home? Where can

you park your truck when you get home? Will you leave it at a truck stop? How far is the closest truck stop?

18. Are the dedicated routes night driving routes? How many drops? **This is a secret the companies don't want you to know.** The best route is steady daytime hours and has the fewest drops. It doesn't matter if you get another $10 or so for each drop. It wastes time.

19. How long would I have to wait to get a dedicated route?

20. What are the requirements needed to get a dedicated route?

21. Will I get my own truck or will I have to share it with another driver?

22. What is your drop and hook percentage? A higher percentage is better. That means less wasted time. When you drop and hook, you aren't waiting around.

23. What areas of the country do you service? What choices do you offer in terms of routes, i.e. All 48 states, west of the Mississippi, the Northeast, and the Southwest? Will I be able to avoid New York City? Is it possible to drive only in the southern part of the country to avoid winter weather?

24. Are your trailers refrigerated? Refrigerated trailers are more of a hassle than dry loads because you have to monitor the refer unit to make sure that it is working properly and make sure that the refer diesel fuel tank is kept relatively full. It's not a huge deal, but it is a factor that you could use to decide between companies if all other things were equal.

25. How long will I have to go out on the road with a trainer?

26. What will I get paid during training? Ask how many weeks of training are required, and how much will you be paid during training.

27. After training will I drive on my own? Or will I have to spend more time as an apprentice? If so, how long? Most long-haul companies will train you for three weeks. But if they require you to go out longer as an apprentice, this can be a very trying experience with little or no redeeming value. Often the apprenticeship is a case of the blind leading the blind. You will be sent out with a relatively new lease driver who can't drive much better than you can. The program is really a financial incentive for drivers to lease a truck because they will make more money when you help them drive their truck.

28. Do you pay for lumpers? Lumpers load and un-load the trailers. If you get a local route, you will probably have to do your own lumping. But long-haul drivers should have paid lumpers. Also ask if the trucking company has an account with the lumpers. Then you won't have to deal with paying lumpers. Do you have to write checks and try to convince the lumpers to accept checks? Do you have to pay with cash? Will the company reimburse you or do you have to pay for your own lumpers? Best is drop and hook. Then you don't have to deal with lumpers and payment for lumpers.

CHAPTER 7
Over-the-Road Training

THE NEXT PHASE OF MY TRAINING was to go out over the road with a trainer. As a female, I was concerned that a male trainer would not respect my boundaries. I had heard some very scary stories from my room-mates. They told me about many women who were beaten and raped by their trainers. The danger was very real.

I voiced my concerns with the placement coordinator. This paid off. My trainer was sent to me from heaven. On Thursday, I began training by going out on the road with a great guy who had been training students for six years. Matt had the whole system figured out. He knew exactly how to do everything so that he was making the maximum amount of dollars that was humanly possible.

Tip: If you want to make a lot of money driving a truck, and you have the patience to wait for six months until you qualify to be a trainer and can implement your plan, follow Matt's example. Study him carefully.

Tip: Before going out with a trainer, talk to the placement coordinator.

The secret to his success was his attention to others. Matt had thought everything through. Matt was very personable, and never once raised his voice to me, even when I know I must have been trying his patience. Everywhere we went, people greeted him warmly by name. I would guess that this single trait of having a fabulous personality guaranteed 98% of Matt's success. He kept a little tiny notebook in his shirt pocket with the names and phone numbers of EVERYONE, EVERYWHERE with whom he ever had dealings. When he called them, he would warmly greet them by name and chit-chat first for a few minutes.

Matt had a good relationship with the placement coordinator who assigned him his trainees. I read the Qualcomm message Karen sent him about me. She told him that she had found a great student for him who would not give him any trouble. When I was almost finished with my training, Karen assigned a new trainee to Matt. This trainee had started training with another trainer, but they didn't get along. She sent Matt a message telling him that this new trainee was a nice kid who didn't get a fair shake with his last trainer. She ended the message with, "You Rock!" I think that she was secretly in love with Matt. From what I saw, I came to the conclusion that a lot of women were secretly in love with Matt!

He had a great relationship with his leasing manager. It did not surprise me that Matt had leased one of the finest trucks known to mankind. His brand new Freightliner Cascadia got excellent mileage (over 7 mpg consistently). Miles per gallon is a big consideration for a lease driver. Driving a fuel-efficient vehicle is crucial to how much money is made. Most trucks get around 6 mpg. By getting an extra mile per gallon, you can save a TON of money on fuel! I absolutely loved that Cascadia. Comfortable and quiet inside, it was a dream to drive. I slept like a baby in the Cascadia. You can see a picture of the cab of Matt's Cascadia on the front cover. When Matt got his first paycheck after leasing the truck, he immediately spotted a discrepancy between what he was told he would be charged and what was actually being deducted from his pay. He called up the leasing company, chatted with the receptionist, Sharon, for ten minutes and then asked to speak with the manager, Henry. They also chit-chatted and then Matt got down to the business of the monthly payment discrepancy. Henry explained his rationale for the discrepancy. Henry said that was the way they had been doing it for years and that that was the way they would continue to do it. Matt pulled out his contract with the leasing company and read a few clauses to Henry. By the time Matt had finished speaking with Henry; Henry had decided to drop all the excess charges.

Everyone in the dedicated division loved Matt. Matt was one of those lucky ones with a lucrative dedicated route that I was telling you about earlier. His route was fabulous! His was the most coveted dedicated route of all. With his trainee as a team member, his truck would cover the route in five days. He took two days off at home in Portland each week. Sweet! And guess what! The girls working at the shipping and receivers loved Matt! They always expedited his paperwork.

He drove a huge amount of highway miles each week by driving from one corner of the country to the other and back, Portland, Oregon to Atlanta, Georgia. Other than Lincoln, Nebraska, his route didn't go through any other big cities. He skirted Portland and Atlanta easily. It was drop and hook—no muss, no fuss. It would never take more than a half hour to drop the load and hook up to another load. The freight was dry, so there was no need to worry about the refer unit. The route featured a spectacularly beautiful stretch of highway through the Columbia River canyon with a view of Mt. Hood. Can you imagine how this fairytale route became his? You're right! The girls in the dedicated division loved Matt!

He had all this and a good love relationship, too! He maintained a good relationship with his wife, Sandy, by being there for her two days out of every week. Matt went to great lengths to spend quality time with her and their two dogs. They scooted around Portland on motor bikes and ate at all their favorite restaurants. Matt called her every day when he was out on the road. They adored each other. Sandy was fiercely loyal to him. Once when one of Matt's trainees did not finish his training with Matt, she went over to the doughnut shop where this guy had started working and really cussed him out. That would teach him to mess around with her man!

I was glad that Matt was a married man who totally respected my physical boundaries. And Matt was glad that I was a happily married woman who would respect HIS boundaries! We had an understanding!

Boundaries are an extremely important factor in determining the success of the training process. He told me that once he had a female trainee who would try to seduce him. He ordered her to keep her clothes on when the curtain was open. He told her that if she did not comply, he would throw her off the truck at the nearest greyhound station.

Matt was doing quite well for himself financially. In addition to the fuel savings his Cascadia gave him, his route took him mostly on the freeway with little city driving. This maximized fuel savings even more. Matt's pay rate was pretty high because he had been driving for five years. But as a trainer, he was able to get paid at that same high rate for every mile that his truck drove. So with me doing half the driving, he made almost twice what he could make driving by himself. He did have to pay me a small token amount of $350 a week.

He only took one week of vacation time each year at Christmas. He was able to get family health insurance for a reasonable cost through his wife's company. He minimized the possibility of his trainees wrecking his truck by only allowing them to drive between pre-arranged mile markers. While he slept, he would only allow me to drive on stretches that were super-easy. That way he was maximizing his safety, as well as insuring that I did not ruin his clutch, transmission, and brakes. I only drove through a city occasionally (Lincoln), and only when he was awake to help me out. Because of these precautions, he had no unusual maintenance expenses.

Before he slept, Matt would tell me to wake him up at a certain mile marker. The mile marker would come right before a big hill or some other difficult driving of some sort. This guy was amazing because I would have to wake him up every two or three hours at least. Then he would guide me through the difficult stretch.

How in the world can somebody get by on that kind of choppy sleep schedule? I could not do that. I need 9 hours in a row to feel right. I could not wake up so often to make sure that everything's OK with my trainee on the difficult stretches of the highway. That guy really earned his money.

But waking up frequently insured his success with his trainees. By training them how to shift properly and brake properly on difficult stretches, he was avoiding the problems of his trainees ruining his clutch, transmission, and brakes. And he was insuring our safety, as well. He was also developing brownie points with God, or good Karma.

This is a secret the trucking companies don't want you to know. One of the most important contributors to Matt's income was through the company's incentive program. He was paid a half a cent a mile for every mile that any of his trainees ever drove for the rest of their driving career as company drivers as long as they stayed with the company, IF they made it through the training with HIM. If they chose to drive a lease truck, he would get one whole cent for every mile that they drive for the rest of their days with the company. In essence, he was getting a commission. Matt had been getting a new student at least every three weeks for the last five years. If he got a student who had completed a week or two with another trainer, he would only have them for a week or two instead of the whole three weeks. That way he would earn his commission more quickly. He had an agreement with the placement coordinator that he would take students who didn't make it with their first or second or third trainer. This was a win-win for both the training coordinator and Matt. She could assure these poor, disenchanted souls that their next trainer would not give them any grief. And Matt would get them through the last week or two and get his commission quicker. Matt was averaging about 20 students a year. He had been doing this for five years before I trained with him. So he had trained about 100 students. He had a reputation for being able to get almost any student through the training because he was so easy-going. Everybody liked Matt. After each student finished training, he insisted that they keep in touch, as each one was one of his "kids."

Let's guesstimate that each of Matt's 100 "kids" averaged about 100,000 miles with the company before they quit. That is not a lot of miles in truck driver miles. Then let's say that 75% became lease drivers and 25% became company drivers.

In this scenario, 75 of the students leased and he made one cent a mile for each of their 100,000 miles. 100,000 miles X $.01 is $1000 that he made for each student who went on to lease a truck from the company. So he made $75,000 from total of 75 students who later became lease drivers.

Then he made a half cent a mile for each of the students who became company drivers. A half cent times 100,000 miles average comes out to $500 for each of them. Multiply $500 by 25 company drivers. He made $12,500 from the students who became company drivers.

Adding the lease drivers to the company drivers, he received a total of $87,500 as a bonus for his efforts to persuade students to stay with the company and to lease. Now, over the course of three weeks, what company do you think Matt would advise you to work for? You guessed it. And do you think that Matt would encourage you to go company or lease? You guessed right again!

This is a secret the trucking companies don't want you to know. Think about all this extra money that Matt is getting from the company as a bonus for his students who completed training with him. It's a lot of money! How can the company afford to pay this money out? They can afford to pay out this money by paying less to their drivers than is paid by other companies.

A further twist in the plot comes when you realize that the trainer will only get these bonuses as long as he remains with the company. This is how they have hooked Matt into their whole scheme. Matt told me that he had been offered very lucrative offers from other companies, but he would not switch companies.

When Matt was awake, I received a lot of instruction about how to shift, center the truck on the road, and drive as fast as possible without ever risking a speeding ticket. The only problem was that I only practiced backing up for about an hour one Saturday. Matt had different excuses each week-end for not giving me my backing practice time.

This was good for him, because he was not taking any risk of me backing into something. The hours that should have been spent teaching me to back up were instead spent at home. But not learning to back up in my training was bad for me, because backing is a critical skill that must be learned. I never really learned how to back up until I got my own truck. Then I finally spent a lot of time perfecting the skill. It was not uncommon for me to spend a half hour each time I need to back up in order to back into the slot or dock perfectly centered and square.

One of Matt's greatest strengths was the ability to wake up every couple of hours. I guess Matt was used to waking up at odd hours from his army days. A West Point graduate, Matt had fought in Desert Storm and other conflicts. Sometimes when I would wake him up, he would bolt out of the bunk with his eyes wide open with an expression of shock. He would not be able to understand where he was for five minutes or so.

It seems to me that a lot of veterans are truck drivers. It seems to appeal to them for some reason. I guess truck driving is similar to the military in a lot of ways. There is a lot of excitement and a lot of risk. If you let your guard down for a minute, you could roll the truck on a curve, or you could top the trailer on a low bridge. You have to be on your toes or you're dead. You often have to get up at ridiculous hours. As in the military, a driver is always moving around, with no need to establish many lasting relationships. The job is very regimented. You need to go where they want you to go when they tell you to go there. And just as in the military, a driver is faced with daily challenges.

During my two days a week off, I spent my time studying the driving modules given to me by the company. I took tests on each module and sent in my answers on the Qualcomm. With Matt's help, I answered every question correctly and was ready to move on to the next phase of my truck driver training. After driving with him for three weeks, Matt dropped me off back at school again and picked up his new trainee. I spent three more days in class completing my first upgrade. During this upgrade we spent nine hours a day learning about how to be successful as a lease driver. This was unpaid.

I then spent 30 more unpaid days at home waiting for my next assignment. The company told me that I had to drive as a team with a lease driver for three weeks. Most people did not have to wait to do this. But, since I am a non-smoker, it took that long to find a lease driver who did not smoke.

I used the time to add the haz-mat and the doubles and triples endorsements to my license. I decided to get these endorsements to make myself more attractive to potential employers. To get the haz-mat endorsement, I had to pay $89 for a background check of my fingerprints. A week later a letter came in the mail confirming that I was not a terrorist. I took it to the DMV and easily passed the endorsement tests.

If I had been smart, I would have used the 30 days to look for a job with another company. Instead, I went back to school and was assigned to the lease truck of Tyrone. The first thing Tyrone did was to tell me that the only rule he had on his truck was that there were no rules.

Immediately, a red flag went up in my mind. Everybody has rules. If they don't tell you what they are, that means you will have to figure out what they are through trial and error.

And so it was. Unfortunately for me, Tyrone was not respectful of my boundaries. I assumed that by telling him that I was a happily married woman, he would understand that the relationship between him and me would be strictly of a business nature.

My assumption was dead wrong. Even though I was older than his mother, Tyrone repeatedly made passes at me. This made me very uncomfortable, as I never felt 100% safe. It was a huge blunder on his part. When I rebuffed him, he would go into somber mood, not speaking to me much for days. Tyrone considered himself to be quite the Casanova. His ego was crushed when I reinforced my need for personal boundaries. I repeatedly explained to him that our relationship was strictly business and that he would just have to accept that.

Tyrone also blew up at me one day when he realized that I did not have enough hours left to deliver the load. I had warned him two days earlier that I was running low on hours. He collected my logs each day in order to put them into the Trip-Pak, so he should have been aware of it. Anyway, when I finally ran out of hours, he had to call his driver manager (DM) and get the load transferred to another driver while we rested.

It really irked him that I was not doing "creative" logging. As he was paid at his pay rate for all the miles his truck drove, this uncooperativeness to fudge my logs prevented him from making more money. Again, after the initial anger, I got the cold treatment. I explained to him that if he was unhappy with my logs, then he should let me know how to correct the problem. Once he realized that nobody had ever clued me in on "creative' logging, he calmed down and explained to me how drivers are able to drive more hours than they are actually logging.

Another time, Tyrone didn't like where I pulled over to change drivers. This earned me the privilege of witnessing another huge temper tantrum and another two days of his suppressed rage.

Later on I did take a class from my company for people who have many log violations. I didn't have any log violations, but I wanted to understand the way the company computer calculated violations. In this class they spell it out for you a bit more. They tell you what you can and cannot do on your logs.

The real bummer about the whole apprenticeship program was that they had told me in school I would spend THREE weeks as an apprentice on a lease truck. This was also spelled out on the internet site. But when I actually got in the truck to begin my team assignment, somehow the requirement had been changed to FOUR weeks! This really made me mad. I had put up with a lot of abuse from this company already, but this was just ridiculous. That was a long four weeks.

I did learn some valuable driving skills during this time, but it was very aggravating for me being cooped up with Tyrone. In retrospect, I should have gone to work for a different company after getting my CDL or after going out with my trainer. I was happy with my CDL training, but after that I put up with a lot of abuse from my company.

Remember the commission my trainer got for the miles later driven for the company by his students? Tyrone got the same deal for his team members! Guess what company he would urge you to work for? Yup. Do you think he would have a bias about whether you go company or lease? You guessed it! So for the whole four weeks, I tolerated an undercurrent of how great it is working for this company and that leasing a truck is the way to go.

Anyway, after I finally finished the apprentice ordeal, I spent a few days at home and then went back to school for three more unpaid days and a second upgrade. The second upgrade was the final brainwashing to lease a truck.

There were ten people in my class. I was the only one who chose to be a company driver. The rest chose to lease.

As the instructor went over the material, ironically I was the only one who could answer the questions. The other students were out in leasing la-la land someplace. I guess they were thinking about how they would show off their beautiful big truck to their friends at home. They were the ones who needed to know how to run their trucking business, not me. It was quite apparent to me that the people who leased were, in reality, the least likely people to succeed.

On the third day of this latest brainwashing, they rounded us up and took us down to the leasing office. We sat around a big conference table and watched a movie about how great it would be once we were behind the wheel of that wonderful lease truck. Then an attractive young woman came in with contracts for us all to sign.

Mind you, I had told the company at least a dozen times and even written it out for them that I had absolutely no interest in leasing a truck. She presented the contract to me last, of course. She didn't want the others to see me refuse it. So I shoved it back at her and sat back to wait. These guys who had all signed the lease papers were sitting there with these stupid grins on their faces. I really felt sorry for them.

This is another secret that the company doesn't want you to know. The statistics showed that 90% of these new lease drivers would forfeit on their leases before the lease expired (even if it was only for six months).

Let's look next at different reasons for driving for the company, leasing, or driving independent.

CHAPTER 8
Company, Lease or Independent?

BEFORE I GO INTO MORE DETAIL, I want you to promise me just one thing. If you think that you might want to lease a truck, just WAIT SIX MONTHS!

Tip: DO NOT LEASE A TRUCK FOR AT LEAST SIX MONTHS!   The company may try to entice you to lease right away after you have finished your training. They may tell you that they have a special deal for new drivers where they will give you a short lease of only six months. Do not accept the bait.

This is another secret that the company doesn't want you to know about.

The company knows that most of the lease drivers will default on their lease within the first few months. When a driver can't make his payments, the company will get their truck back and the ex-driver will still owe them for the rest of the lease payments on the contract. Then they can turn around and lease the same truck to another unsuspecting victim.

The problem with leasing a truck right away is that a new driver will make lots of mistakes. He will have fender benders and will run over stop signs on tight turns. Some new drivers roll the rig and top the trailer. If you are a lease driver, you will have to pay for any damages out of your own pocket. But as a company driver, the company will pay. When you turn in your lease truck, they go over it with a fine-toothed comb looking for any damage that they can put on your bill. They never even look at a company truck when you quit.

A new driver still doesn't know if he will want to keep driving a truck for very long. If you have leased, you are stuck with those payments even if you quit driving. As a company driver, if you decide trucking is not for you, you can just walk away and say goodbye, no strings attached. If you become disenchanted with the company and decide to switch companies, it's the same thing. The lease driver can't walk away from the payments he has contracted to pay. It also takes time to learn how to deal with your DM, and how to maximize your efforts to make money. As a lease driver, you can't afford any weeks of low pay, because your truck payment is so ridiculously high. If you are stuck in Laredo with no load out, you won't even be able to make your truck payment, let alone feed your family.

If you drive company for six months, you will be eligible to become a trainer. THEN, as a trainer, if you decide to lease, you will be able to make a lot more money because you will be getting paid for all the miles your truck drives, including the miles that your student drives, less a small weekly salary you will pay to your trainee. Once you become a trainer, you will be much less likely to default on your lease, because you will be making a lot more money. The company also gives trainers better loads with more miles and less stops. Just remember to take the driving precautions with your student that we talked about before. If your student damages your truck and you are a lease driver, you will pay for needed repairs.

Company drivers have no truck expenses, can get benefits, and are eligible for promotions. The company pays for fuel, maintenance, repairs, everything. Company drivers can get a 401K, health, dental, and vision benefits and are eligible for promotions to other positions in the company. Lease drivers have to pay all their own expenses, do not get benefits, and are not eligible for promotions. New lease drivers have no idea of how much they will be making until they actually lease the truck and start driving. They have no idea of how high their expenses will be. These new lease drivers will soon discover that they have to drive a LOT of miles to even break even on their paychecks after the company is through taking out a gigantic chunk in deductions.

It's tough for a new lease driver to make the lease payments at the same time as they are still learning how to drive a truck efficiently. Most new lease drivers default on their lease after a month or two. The fact is that when you break your lease because you can't keep up with the payments, your credit will be hurt badly. Company drivers can later choose to lease. Lease drivers cannot choose to go back to working for the company.

Most of the reasons that the company gives you to entice you to lease instead of drive for the company are really lame. Two lame reasons to lease are that you can take your pet with you and that you can choose the color of your truck.

Some companies have a rule that you cannot take your pet with you in your truck if you are a company driver. Or they may tell you that you must pay a huge deposit if you take your pet. If you like to follow their rules, this could be a problem. Your company may tell you that only lease drivers can have pets in their trucks. I know many, many people who have leased a truck for this reason alone!

But lease drivers are not the only ones who have pets in their trucks. I know many drivers who take pets in their company trucks. They never paid any deposit either.

This is another secret that the company doesn't want you to know. The company doesn't know if you have your pet in your truck anyway. You are out on your own all the time. Even company drivers who work dedicated routes out of a central headquarters have pets in their trucks. Nobody cares a bit. Out there on the road alone, many drivers, especially women, feel much safer with their dog beside them. I met a company driver's cat who likes to talk on the CB, sleeps in the compartment above the dash, and hangs out the window to greet the security guards at the gate. This cat had lived in a company driver's truck for years. Who cares if you take your pet with you in your company truck? This is not a criminal offense. Some people even have three dogs with them. Not being allowed to take a pet with you in a company truck should NOT be used as a reason to lease. If you are a company driver, just take your pet with you. What your company doesn't know won't hurt them.

They tell you that you can choose the color of truck you want if you lease. This is not always true. If the color you want is not available, you may have to wait for quite a while. I know many lease drivers who did not want to have to wait for their favorite color. So they just took the standard color that was available. They didn't want to have to wait for extended periods of time for their favorite color. Wanting to drive a different color truck is just a desire to appease your ego anyway.

This is another secret that the company doesn't want you to know. When a company truck pulls into a weigh station, the company driver is very rarely asked to pull over for an inspection of his truck. As a rule, the inspectors only choose to inspect lease trucks but not company trucks because they know that the company makes sure that their company trucks are maintained properly. But lease drivers don't want to have to pay for needed repairs and will often neglect proper maintenance. Lease drivers are an easy target for fines. The inspectors can tell if you are driving a company or lease truck by the number on the front fender of the truck. In my company, the lease trucks start with a different digit than the company trucks.

I was pulled over and subjected to an inspection at a weigh station when I was driving Tyrone's lease truck. It was an ordeal that I do not care to repeat. The reason I was pulled into the weigh station in the first place was because the trailer was overweight on the rear axle.

Tyrone had neglected to weigh his truck after leaving the shipper. He told me that the truck was not overweight. He based this decision on his dashboard gauge which showed the weight on the shocks. This was total hooey. The truth is that lease drivers hesitate to weigh their loads because they will have to pay the scale fee.

The only way to know if your load is overweight is to actually WEIGH it. Tyrone did not want to weigh the load because that would cost him $7 or $8. A company driver would be reimbursed for scale fees, but a lease driver has to pay the cost out of his own pocket.

First, I endured the 45 minute inspection. Then I wrestled with the rusted tandems to move them back in order to take some weight off the rear. Finally, I ended up with a stern warning and a warning ticket.

I was put through this inconvenience because I was driving a lease truck and because the lease truck had not been weighed immediately after leaving the shipper. If I were to be pulled over at that weigh station again in that same truck and an inspector found something wrong again, then I would get a fine and points on my license.

As a company driver, I was never inspected. I was just waved through hundreds of weigh stations with a smile. After showing my registration papers the first time at a weigh station, they will never ask me again. I just drive right on by.   Of course, I always weigh my loads immediately after leaving the shipper and adjust my tandems at that time if need be. It's so much easier that way! When your load is not overweight, the highway weight sensors register that you are not overweight. The sensors on the highway weigh your load as you drive past, even at top speed. When they sense that your weight is fine, you will usually get the green light on your dashboard allowing you to pass the weigh station without having to stop.

Now when somebody is trying to get you to do something in such a persistent manner, it is time to wonder why. Why does the company persistently push us to lease? We have talked about how they take advantage of those who default on their leases. What does the company have to gain in the time before a lease driver defaults?

This is another secret that the company doesn't want you to know. The secret is that the company will have a license to steal from your paycheck. In class they brainwash you into thinking that all of the myriad deductions are quite reasonable, but it is not true. I know lease drivers who actually get negative paychecks! They owe the company more and more money as time goes on! If you lease, there will be a whole lot of incidental charges taken out of your check.

If you lease your own truck, (read "rent" your own truck) you will be responsible for a huge lease payment every week. YOU pay for the fuel, even when you get lost and drive a long way out of the way. The company helps with the fuel, but it is still a huge expense for a lease driver.

And remember also that many companies aren't paying you for actual miles driven between destinations. They are paying for a much shorter distance, akin to what a crow would fly straight between destinations. The lease driver is paying for the gas for actual miles driven and being paid for a much smaller number of miles.   If you lease, you will not have the option of getting the company's group health insurance and other benefits because you are not employed by the company. Instead, you are an independent contractor. If you want health insurance, you must pay for it yourself, and it will be expensive. The older you are, the more expensive it will be. If you or your dependents have any pre-existing health problems, you will be out of luck. Unlike most group insurance offered to company drivers, the insurance a lease driver buys will not cover pre-existing problems at all. A lease driver may have to take a physical exam before getting insurance. The insurance may be super-expensive if your health is not so great. Or the insurance company may refuse to insure you altogether.

When your truck breaks, YOU will pay for the repairs. When you need tires, chains, or anything else, YOU will pay for them. You will run yourself ragged trying to drive enough miles just to break even.

Do you have family? Forget about seeing them. You won't have time to go home. Good luck trying to make enough money to feed them. I know many lease drivers whose checks are, at most, $100 a week. The majority of lease drivers end up defaulting on their lease. You really don't want to go there.

Lease drivers who do manage to stick it out for the first six months often become trainers in order to make more money. They are paid for all of the miles that their student drives. But they must assume responsibility for paying the student a small fixed amount each week.

This can work out OK if the student doesn't crash the truck, or ruin the clutch, the transmission, the brakes, etc.   Unfortunately, students do all these things with regularity. The repairs can set you back financially for years into the future. So it's a crap shoot. The trainer must sleep while the student is driving. That is a scary proposition. I know of one trainer who died instantly when his neck was broken as he slept. His student driver lost control of the truck on a steep downgrade.

Another way to make more money as a lease driver is to take on a new driver as your apprentice. Some companies offer this as an option as an extra incentive to induce people to lease. **This is another secret that the company doesn't want you to know.** The company's secret is that the apprentice program lengthens the amount of time before a new driver who will become a company driver will get his own truck. This saves the company a lot of money. It also lengthens the time before the company will have to pay the company driver on the company driver pay scale.   And it's another round of brainwashing to persuade them to lease. The company also uses the program to persuade people to lease. When a lease driver gets an apprentice, he can make extra money from the miles the apprentice drives. Being a lease driver who takes on a new driver as a team member is similar to being a trainer, except that the student has already been with a trainer and has three weeks of driving experience. Also, you are not responsible for training the student.

You won't make as much money as a trainer, but the concept is similar. You get paid for all the miles the truck is driven at your pay rate except for 11 or 12 cents a mile that goes to the new driver. Again, you must hope that your team member does not crash your truck or ruin the transmission, brakes, clutch, etc. You are sleeping while the new driver is driving.   I have spoken with a number of lease drivers who, years later, are still trying to pay for the damage done to their truck by their trainees or apprentices.

Lease drivers are running their own business. They have to keep track of all expenses and income. Their taxes are more difficult because they are running their own business.

Tip: If you decide to lease, check out different leasing companies and choose the best deal for the truck that most appeals to you. Truck leasing companies who are not associated with a trucking school may offer you a better deal. Even if you lease elsewhere, you can still choose to work as an independent contractor with the trucking company of your choice.

The company probably has a program that will allow lease drivers to buy fuel for less than the pump price. Don't let this persuade you to lease. Fuel is still a huge expense for lease drivers.

Tip: Try to lease a truck that averages 7 mpg or more. One of the most important factors to consider is the fuel economy of the lease truck.

An independent driver drives his own truck. He is free to act as an independent contractor for a trucking company. Or he can arrange his own loads and contract directly with the shippers to deliver their loads.

I have spoken with many independent drivers. They usually became independent after years of driving for a company as a company driver or a lease driver. Many of them have more than one truck and employ other drivers to drive for them.

In these times of a troubled economy, independents are having a tough time making a go of it. I hear the same thing from all of them. They are just squeaking by.

The upside of being an independent as opposed to a lease driver is that your truck payments are actually going toward buying the truck. Lease payments are like paying rent. You are renting the truck. At the end of your lease period, the truck belongs to the leasing company. You will actually own your truck if you become an independent. And, like the lease drivers, you can still be an independent contractor for a company if you want to be.

Employees can give you a lot of grief. If an independent has drivers who drive for his company, he may experience the problem of a driver taking off with his truck and contracting loads for himself. Or maybe his truck gets abandoned. Or perhaps his tractors and trailers have been stolen. Small independents cannot bear these troubling circumstances financially.

Many independents have sold their trucks and gone back to work as company drivers. Then they can be sure that they will get a steady paycheck and be able to take time off to be with their families without being responsible for truck payments.

Tip: Drive for a company for quite a while and get to know the industry before thinking about buying your own truck. If you are thinking about becoming an independent driver, you need a good background in running your own business. These are troubling economic times. Don't put your neck on the line.

CHAPTER 9
Should I Go Solo or Team?

THE NEXT DECISION TO MAKE IS WHETHER TO DRIVE SOLO OR TEAM. This decision, for me, was another no-brainer. I like my privacy. I had struggled through more than enough time driving as a team for seven weeks. I never felt like I had enough room for my food, my clothes, or myself. If you don't mind sharing a small space with another person, you may not mind driving as a team. But it is important to find a compatible team member. As a team, you are always playing musical beds. As a team member, the non-driving member sleeps in the bottom bunk while the driving member drives. So you are both sleeping in the same bed, albeit at different times. When you finish sleeping and are ready to drive, you must move your own stuff up to the top bunk and move the other guy's stuff down to the bottom bunk. There are times when your wheels aren't turning and you are each sleeping in one of the bunks. Then, when one person gets up for any reason, it will probably wake the other one up. If you are the type of person who doesn't mind this situation, you may not mind driving as a team.

I don't like to drive at night. Do you? When you drive as a team somebody has to drive at night, at least some of the time. If you drive as a team, you would have to agree on who drives at night, or agree on sharing that responsibility.

Have you had other roommates in the past? I have. I never got along with any of them. The only person I can get along with in close quarters is my husband. In brief, I need my own space. The small cab of the truck without anybody else in it is challenging enough for me. I would not drive team.

Tip: Is it easy for you to get along with room-mates? If not, make a note in your notebook to drive solo. Circle it and underline it.

If you drive team, you will have to sleep while the truck is moving. For some people, this is very disturbing. They never get a good night's (day's) sleep. I sleep like a baby when the truck is moving, but I still would not drive as a team. I sleep like a baby when the truck is not moving, too. Therefore, this is not a factor for me. I want to stop when I am tired and sleep. I don't want to have to drive because my partner wakes me up and tells me it is my turn. I like to sleep when my body needs to sleep. You can't do that when you drive team. I also like to ride my bike around in different places. If I drove team, the truck would not stop long enough for me to do that. It can be difficult to get enough exercise when you are driving team.

You will have a bit more money in your jeans if you drive as a team. The number one reason to drive as a team is that you will get a few more cents a mile than you would if you were to drive solo. This relates to as much as $10,000 a year more for you if you drive team than you would make driving solo. This is not worth it to me. Nothing would be worth it to me. Is it worth it to you?

You may like sharing the responsibility of getting the load there on time. If you don't like to drive as many miles as your partner, driving team could be financially advantageous to you. When you are both awake, the non-driving partner can take care of tasks that need to be done, like sending messages and filling out trip-paks. Cooking and cleaning can be shared.

Some people don't like to be alone. Driving as a team suits these types of people well. Do you prefer to be around someone else all the time? Make a note to drive team if you prefer companionship. Finding a compatible partner is the key to making it work. If you do decide to drive team, it is crucial that you find a partner with whom you are compatible. Perhaps you already know another driver with whom you would like to team. The company probably has a "matchmaker" who can help you find a compatible partner. The most important issues are to find someone who smokes or doesn't smoke and to find someone who is neat or sloppy. If your nose is sensitive, look for someone with good hygiene. You should have similar ideas about how long and how often you want to go home. If you both live in the same area, it simplifies things immensely.

Tip: Decide as early as possible if you want to drive solo or team. If you think you might want to drive team, start looking for a partner when you go to CDL School. Check out your roommates and classmates for a potential compatible partner. Look for someone as much like you as possible, i.e., smoker/non-smoker, neat/messy, vegetarian/meat-eater, and so forth. Look for someone with similar tastes in music, videos, magazines, books, hobbies, and sports. Talk to your roommates and find out if they know anybody who they think might be a good match for you. If you identify someone as a possible team partner, find out their feelings on the matter. If there is any interest, get to know that person as well as you can. Decide as soon as possible if you think that it wouldn't work, and move on. Make notes about what you like and dislike about potential partners and try to find a partner with qualities you like.

If you like your privacy, as a solo driver, you've got it. There is rarely a need to speak with anyone if you don't want to. On the other hand, it can get mighty lonely out there. Driving solo, you will decide when and where your truck will go. You will choose when to stop for breaks and when to sleep. You will choose which loads to accept. You will choose which route to take. You will choose how and when to exercise. You will choose when to shop and when to prepare meals and eat. You will choose when to take home time and when to take vacations. You will not have to agree or argue with a team member. You will wake and sleep when you want to. If you don't want to drive at night, you can avoid driving at night. The same goes for bad weather. It's all your call. But for all this independence, you will be paid a bit less. To me, it is well worth it. But I am extremely independent.

After my final refusal to lease, I was signed on as a solo company driver and taken to meet my driver manager (DM). He told me that I could pick up my truck later that afternoon. I got the truck number and the keys. Then, by chance, I ran into an old pal, Kim, who told me that the truck I was getting had been hers. Kim was quitting because her DM would never allow her to go home. She requested home time repeatedly and was repeatedly refused. Even when she had a medical problem that required a visit to her physician, her DM refused to let her keep the appointments. Kim had the same DM that I was getting. Uh-oh! Kim was a hard worker who never delivered a load late. She had driven awful routes in awful weather. She repeatedly drove into New York City (UGH!) when she was given a load assignment that went there. Kim was really a model driver. But because of her good nature, she was constantly taken advantage of by the company. She was used and abused. Kim told me that the only thing she would miss about working for this company was this truck. Company trucks are supposed to be governed at 60 mph. This one was governed at 68 mph. Remember, the faster you can go, the faster you can make money. She warned me never to service it at the company's repair shop because they would set the governor back to 60. She clued me in on the other little quirks of this truck and gave me a few things to go with it, like a car vacuum, the carpets, curtains, and some miscellaneous food items.

As a company driver, all my extras were free. I went to the parts department and picked up new chains, light bulbs, glad hand seals, and jumper cables. I traded in my fire extinguisher for a freshly-charged one. The lease drivers had to buy all these things. The chains alone cost them $200. After fueling her up, I was on my way home for my promised 3 days of home time. After driving all night, I arrived home exhausted. It was Friday afternoon. My DM called me up and told me to go pick up a load and deliver it 1000 miles away. I told him that I had just gotten home. He was unsympathetic. I was angry. I thought about it for a bit. Then I sent in a Qualcomm message refusing the load because I was going to take the home time that had been promised to me.

On Monday afternoon, my DM finally noticed that I had not taken the load. He was furious. He called me up and screamed at me that I had abandoned a load and could be fired for that. I calmly told him that I had not abandoned a load, because I had never accepted the load. In fact I had REFUSED the load. I told him to read the Qualcomm message I had sent on Friday. I did not care if I was fired. I knew he was a selfish person who would never let people take their home time, and I wanted him to know that he could not push me around. I told him that I would be ready to drive on Wednesday, and not to call me until then. Interestingly enough, on Wednesday when he called, his mood had changed. All of a sudden it was, "Let's let bygones be bygones and let's start over." I guess he got a reprimand from his superiors about the way he was doing his job. Good! Now we had an understanding. The company was tired of losing company drivers because their DM would not give them their home time.

So I excitedly set out on my first load assignment. I was sent to pick up a load of meat in Dodge City, Kansas and to deliver it in Laredo, Texas. I followed the directions I had received on the Qualcomm, and drove around Dodge City for two hours looking for this mysterious shipper. I finally asked about the shipper at a truck stop and discovered that the name of the shipper that my company had provided was an old name used years ago. So I finally got the load. The trailer doors had broken hinges. I took the load to a nearby scale and found that it was overweight on the rear axle. I tried to move the tandems and found that they were rusted shut. I took the rig into a repair shop to fix the tandems and the doors. The manager spent three hours on the phone waiting for a repair authorization from my company's service shop. He never got it and finally went home at 6 p.m. My company's service shop was just terrible about getting back with authorizations. Then one of the guys in the repair shop stopped on the way to his car and (out of the goodness of his heart) showed me a trick to free the tandems. He switched the connections on the trailer brakes and then had me rock the trailer back and forth a bit until the tandems finally moved. Again, being female sometimes has its advantages.

I didn't have a lot of time to deliver the load when I started, but now I was hopelessly behind schedule. I Qualcommed my situation to my company and then drove continuously to my destination, where I arrived an hour late. Even though it was not my fault, I had begun my driving career with a late load on my record. Bummer!

When I got my first paycheck, I noticed that I was not getting my safety bonus of one extra cent per mile. I had been watching the safety videos, attending classes at the school, and passing quizzes. I then read the fine print on the pay scale and noticed that the safety bonus was already included in the pay advertised. So if I had not kept up with the safety videos, I would have been getting one cent less per mile than what was shown on the pay scale.

I drove solo over-the-road throughout the forty-eight states for another six weeks. I made about $600 a week. Then right before my ninety-day mark from the day I was first hired, I applied for a dedicated route. I wanted to be able to go home each night. I was told that I could start right away. I asked the dedicated division office to call my DM and ask him to give me the home time I had requested three weeks earlier. Miraculously, my DM sent me home. I think he was glad to get rid of me. Now he could get a new driver that would put up with his bullying.

I spent a few days at home and then started the dedicated route. I drove my truck to the headquarters of the company division of my new dedicated route. There I was assigned to ride along with one of the other drivers while he did his route. I was told that I would receive $100 for that day on my next paycheck. The route involved picking up a loaded refrigerated trailer at the shipper and then delivering it to three different grocery stores in the same day. The route involved a lot of city driving and a lot of waiting around at shippers. When I got my next paycheck, I noticed that I had not been paid the $100 for the day when I rode along to be introduced to the route. I called my supervisor and asked her why I had not been paid for that day. She said that she would check on it. Translation, "You actually believed that we were going to pay you?" I was never paid for that day. I had to buy a car because my hometown would not let me park my tractor within the city limits. I ended up driving my car 30 miles each way to and from the nearest truck stop to get to my rig.

The route was notorious for horrible weather, including high winds. I was expected to leave home and start my route sometime between 4 p.m. and 1 a.m. I never knew ahead of time when it would be. At 3:30 pm, my supervisor would call me and tell me when I should head out. My route took about 12 hours from the time I left home until I returned. Even though it was great to be home everyday, I could not enjoy it. Sleeping at odd hours during the day left me feeling horrible. I just could not adapt to sleeping in the day. Driving at night was precarious. I continuously drank Red Bulls to try and stay awake. I got one day off per week which I spent sleeping continuously for 24 hours.

At each store where I dropped my load, I spent about an hour or two. I waited to dock, waited to be unloaded, monitored the merchandise being unloaded, and raised the trailer door and refer compartment doors. I also had to monitor the refer compartments' temperatures.

The real kicker was the size of my paychecks. Even though my pay was raised from 26 cents per mile to 34 cents per mile, and I was working longer than ever each day, my pay had dropped from about $600 per week after deductions when I was driving long haul to just $150 - $200 a week on this dedicated route. And I was putting up with way more aggravation. I drove this route for three weeks. As my husband was scheduled for surgery in three more weeks, I needed to keep my insurance. But I sure as heck wasn't going to keep driving this crummy route. I didn't want to go back to the long haul, because I couldn't stand being away from my husband any more. So I called my boss and told him I was going to take a 30-day leave of absence. He told me that if I was not back in 30 days, I would automatically be terminated. I then called my company's insurance department. Lo and behold the insurance department supervisor answered the phone! Shock! She told me to send a check for the cost of one month's health insurance. Then we would still be covered during the leave of absence.

CHAPTER 10
The Money and Everything Else

YOU WILL NOT MAKE A LOT OF MONEY for a while. You will have to pay your tuition in a lump sum up front or else sign with a finance company to pay it off gradually. You may be paying between $3000 and $5000 for tuition at the beginning of your CDL training. Sure, you can put it on your credit card or finance the whole thing. But those payments will be coming due and you will either have to pay them or watch your debt escalate and your credit deteriorate. If you choose to finance the tuition through the school's finance company, you will end up paying a LOT more. The companies lure you in by assuring you that your tuition will be reimbursed. But very few people ever drive long enough with the company who trains them to get reimbursed for their tuition. They move on to a better company long before this happens. Think of that tuition money as your own money that will become history the minute you sign the contract with the finance company or pay it with your credit card or cash or check.

The time needed to get your CDL could be as little as two weeks or as long as six months. You will not be paid during this time. After you complete your CDL, it may take some time to find a company that can best meet your needs and begin with them. This is unpaid time.

When you go out with your trainer, you will make about $350 a week or so. If you can get a reasonable trainer, you can get through the training in just three weeks. Then you must attend your company's upgrade for three more days (unpaid) and make your way home to get your CDL transferred to your home state. This may take a week or two which is unpaid.

If your company requires you to drive as a team with a lease driver, you will probably have to wait for another unpaid period of time before you go out on the road and start earning money again. I waited for a month. When I teamed with a lease driver, I was paid 12 cents a mile for every mile that the truck drove. One week, my truck drove about 7000 miles a week. That week my gross pay was almost $800, less $200 in taxes and payroll deductions for a $600 paycheck. The other three weeks our truck drove fewer miles, and I made around $600 or so before deductions. After $200 in deductions, I made about $400 a week. After a month of driving team with a lease driver I attended a second unpaid upgrade.

When you become a solo driver or are driving with your own team (two of you) over the road, most company drivers will make $500-$800 a week, more or less. I made 26 cents per mile to start. I drove about 3000 miles a week. They took out about $200 a week for insurance and taxes. So I was making a bit under $600 a week. Another catch is that the company takes money out of each paycheck to be used to pay for anything that you may owe them when you quit. My company took $20 a week out of my paycheck. After I quit, they said I owed insurance money that I didn't owe, so that they could keep this money. Resistance was futile.

If you look at the pay scales on various companies' websites, you will see that you start out at about 26 or 30 cents per mile as a solo company driver. You will see various cents per mile for different length trips. The shorter the trip, the more cents per mile you are paid. Most trips for a long-haul driver are more than 1000 miles. So the lowest cents per mile that you see on the pay scale is what you will usually be making as a long-haul driver. Then you get periodic raises of a cent or two as you gain experience over time.

Pay scales are meaningless unless you know how many miles a week you will average. Let's say you average 3000 miles a week. (That's pretty good for a solo driver.) If you are working for a company that pays 30 cents a mile for trips over 1000 miles you would be making about $900 a week. Then after they take out $100 for insurance and another $100 in deductions, you would be taking home $700 a week.

But what if business is slow or you have a route with fewer miles? You may only make $300 or less a week. That could be your reality. Team drivers make a few cents more per mile.

The odds are that you will never make enough money driving a truck to even pay off your truck driving school tuition. Most people quit long before they have paid off their tuition.

If you look at pay scales for lease drivers, you will see that they start at about 90 cents per mile. The immediate reaction is to think that lease drivers will make more than company drivers. But you can't tell much from looking at the pay scales for lease drivers because there are too many other variables. Lease drivers have to pay for fuel and all of their own expenses. New lease drivers often make far less money than company drivers because they haven't learned to control their expenses. If you are a lease driver, it is unbelievable how much the company can leach from your paycheck.

Tip: You can make more money by becoming a trainer or a lease driver who teams with a new driver. Then you are making money off of the miles that the student or new driver is driving. It is necessary to pay your dues by driving for many months before you can make more money by becoming a trainer. This has its own set of hazards to your finances if your student damages your truck. Good trainers must work very hard to earn their money. Their sleep is short and frequently interrupted.

Tip: After driving for a year or two, you could get a better-paying job driving tankers. As time goes by, your financial horizons can really open up. You might get a job filling propane tanks. You might drive those huge over-sized rigs hauling mobile homes or even windmill vanes. Or you could stumble onto something really fun and lucrative like driving a rock band's equipment around to all the cities on their tour. The demand for experienced drivers is huge.

A. GPS Systems.

I bought a computer program for $75 at Best Buy called DeLorme Street Atlas USA 2009. I put the disc into my laptop and downloaded the program. This computer program comes with a small GPS that connects into a USB port on your computer. You put the GPS on the dash and program your route into the computer. You can upgrade this GPS program on the internet to keep up with road changes. It has lots of options so that you can program it just the way you like. Before setting out on a new load assignment, I program the start and finish as well as each restroom and sleep stop. I also mark all the truck stops, rest areas, and Wal-Marts, so that I will always know where and when I can stop. My current ETA is updated to the second. It shows me my direction of travel and speed. The number of options is mind-boggling. I can watch the course in 3-D if I choose. I have programmed my GPS to alert me visually as well as by voice. I especially like the option that plans the route with or without tolls. I choose to go the shorter, toll-free route when traffic is light, but choose the toll roads to avoid heavy traffic. I chose the voice of Microsoft Mary who gently tells me a mile before, .3 mile before, and right before I am to make a turn. It is music to my ears when I hear her telling me when to turn. She tells me which lane to get in to make the next turn and when to bear left or right. It's a navigator without a bad temper. When I still get off course, Microsoft Mary doesn't say, "I told you three times which turn to take and you still blew it." No. She immediately re-calculates and, without any frustration in her voice, kindly helps me to get on the right course again.

I would not consider the small GPS systems because they are expensive and do not offer the variety of options that I can get with my computer program. My Toshiba Qosmio computer screen is 17 inches with nice Harmon/Kardon speakers. I can also plug the computer it into the truck stereo.

Tip: Program your GPS to alert you of upcoming one-way streets.

Tip: To accommodate and secure your computer, buy a small set of plastic drawers for $9 at Wal-Mart, take out the drawers and secure the plastic frame to the side of the passenger seat (facing the driver's seat) with bungee cords around the bottom and top of the frame. Then bungee the laptop computer onto the top shelf. You can turn your head to the right and see the screen.

Even with a GPS, at times you find yourself in a bad spot. Sometimes the GPS is just plain wrong. Or you didn't listen very well. You get trapped and have to figure out a way to get the truck out of a jam. It is a pain. It is best to avoid a U-turn at all costs. It is dangerous. I will drive many miles out of my way if need be.   Although I could not drive a truck without a GPS, that doesn't mean that everybody needs to have one. If you have an innate sense of direction and can drive while looking at a map, you may not want a GPS.

Tip: Use your common sense if the GPS is telling you to turn down a road that doesn't look like it will accommodate a large truck. Just slow down in the intersection and take a gander down the street before you commit yourself to turn. The GPS will recalculate a new route if you don't turn.

Tip: When you program your route into your GPS, double-check it with the route your company gave you to make sure it matches. If it doesn't, re-route the GPS to match the company route. The route your company gives you is usually safe for trucks. That route will not have low bridges or narrow streets.   And always make sure you have a map to back you up when the GPS leads you astray.

Tip: The best map book is the laminated deluxe Rand-McNally professional driver map book found in most truck stops. Pick up a truck stop book while you're at it.

B. Water.

Tip: Drink a lot of water and take time to stop and use the bathroom. Every process in your body depends on water. It is important to keep your urinary tract in good shape. It is no fun to get a bladder infection. And getting a doctor's appointment and the time to go to the doctor is even harder. Tea or coffee or soda pop is not good enough. Get a five-gallon jug and fill it with reverse-osmosis-filtered water from the dispensers in front of grocery stores. Get two one-liter water bottles. Fill them each morning and afternoon. My water bottles are the Camelback BPA-free type with a spout and a plastic straw. They don't get in the way of my vision when I drink them while I am driving.

It is really important to drink a lot of pure water. I know you don't want to have to stop very often because it will take longer to get your load delivered. But taking care of your health should be your first priority.

C. Danger.

Truck driving is inherently dangerous. If you drive safely and avoid driving in snow, ice, wind, fog, and driving rain, you decrease your chances of getting into an accident. But there will be many times when you must keep driving in adverse conditions in order to deliver your load on time. If you are already on a load when bad weather hits, you still have to get the load there on time, so you'll be stuck driving in the bad weather. Driving in bad weather can be nerve-wracking and dangerous. When driving on slick roads and ice, the danger of jack-knifing is always present. High winds present further danger to trucks. The rig's high profile makes it extremely prone to being blown over, especially when empty. If you regularly drive in and out of Wyoming, you are especially vulnerable to being blown out of your lane or rolling the rig.

Bad weather can also be hazardous to your paycheck. When the weather is too dangerous to drive, you won't be earning any money. In order to make money, your wheels must be turning. The slower they turn, the less money you will make. If your load is late, for whatever reason, your job may be at risk.

There will also be many times when you must drive at night. It is more dangerous. You don't have as many visual cues as you have in the daylight. It is especially tough in the wee hours of the morning when you are really tired.

Driving through big cities can be very frustrating and tiring. I try to enter cities like Dallas, Atlanta, Los Angeles, and St. Louis at about 1 a.m. Then they are a breeze.

You might get "stuck" with a route that takes you out in winter conditions frequently. One way around this might be to find a route where you will drive in a part of the country with nice weather. During nasty winter weather, you could take a leave of absence (unpaid) of up to 30 days without losing your job. If you don't mind suffering the wrath of your DM, you can always just refuse a load. But any way you look at it, even in the southern parts of the country and even in the summer, you will have to drive in bad weather. It's just a question of how often.

D. The dreaded weigh stations.

You must stop at every open weigh station if you do not get a green light on your little weigh station box on your dashboard. Then if the scales show that you have too much weight overall, or in one set of wheels, you must correct it. If you do not stop, you could be in big trouble. The cops may chase you down. Or you will get a ticket the next time you come through.

You may consider weigh stations to be a nuisance. Some drivers who are worried about weigh stations will drive many miles out of their way in order to circumvent them. I have had to stop at as many as six weigh stations in one day. It is time-consuming and stressful. You must have your logs current, as you may be asked to produce today's and the previous six days' logs. If you have made a mistake on any of those logs, you may get a ticket. Serious violations could even land you in jail. You may be told to pull into the inspection area for an inspection of your truck.

Tip: Weigh your truck at the nearest scale after picking up each load. If the load is overweight, you must return it to the shipper immediately. If an axle is overweight, you must move your tandems. It is best to move them immediately after leaving the shipper. If you are prepared, weigh stations won't be a problem for you. If your truck is properly maintained and your load is not too heavy overall or on any one axle, you will not have to worry. Weigh stations just slow you down a bit.

Tip: Make sure your trainer teaches you how to move your tandems. It can often be difficult to move the tandems because they get stuck. Moving the tandems is a learned skill which many drivers have not learned. If you are told to move them at the weigh station and you can't do it, you will be given a ticket and grounded there until your company can send someone out to fix the problem. This is no fun.

E. If your DM won't let you go home...

Your driver manager may make it extremely difficult to get home. Remember, it is not in your driver manager's best interests to let you go home, because he only gets paid when you deliver a load on time. Even if you make it clear to him that home is very important to you, good luck with actually getting him to send you home.

Tip: If you have a problem getting your home time, go over the DM's head to the fleet manager. Request your home time formally on the Qualcomm three weeks before you want it. Driver managers may be fired for denying you home time. This is the main reason why drivers quit, so the companies are serious about getting you your home time. Don't let your DM push you around!

F. Do you have pain?

If you have musculoskeletal problems, they may get worse from the extended hours sitting behind the wheel. I injured my own back and neck in sporting accidents years ago. Driving the truck caused my pain to flare. I was able to get out of pain by seeing a Physician/Rolfer who specializes in chronic pain.

Rolfing is a form of body-work that re-aligns your body to bring it back into line with gravity. It is a very effective means of removing chronic pain permanently. You can find a Rolfer by looking on the internet under "the Rolf Institute" and also under "the Guild for Structural Integration."

I have seen chiropractors and gotten temporary relief. The pain always returned. After I got "Rolfed," the pain was gone and didn't return.

The problem with most medical doctors is that they have never been trained about how to help people actually get rid of their pain. All they understand is pills, needles, and surgery. Stay away from them. Taking pills makes you a dangerous driver and does nothing to actually remove the cause of the pain. Needles are also a temporary fix. Surgery often makes things worse. They may tell you to go to the gym and strengthen. This is also bad advice. If you have rotations in the vertebrae of your spine and you try to strengthen, you will make your problems worse. The correct approach is to first remove the cause of the rotations, then de-rotate the bones, and then rehabilitate with strengthening exercises.

Rolfing addresses the causes of spinal rotations by lengthening shortened tissues that are pulling the bones out of place. Rolfers look at muscular imbalances as a part of imbalances in the whole body. If your back problem originates from a twisted leg, the

Rolfer will first straighten the twist in the leg, then move up to the back. If neck pain originates from a cranial problem caused by head trauma, a Rolfer who has studied cranial sacral therapy will correct the cranial imbalance first, and then relieve problems in the neck.

Tip: If you have pain, it is important to see a specialist who can advise you about what you need to do in order to get better. Do yourself a favor and get the necessary help for your physical problems. Problems just get worse with neglect.

G. When all the truck stops are full...

Tip: Stop driving early in the evening and get a spot as close as possible to the restrooms. Many truck stops and rest areas are full by 9 p.m., especially in the eastern part of the country.

Tip: Plan your drive and drive your plan. Before you go, plan your route on your GPS, or write it down if you don't have a GPS, so that you know where and when you will stop for breaks and where you will sleep.

H. What about CB radios?

Some drivers must have the CB on all the time. I am one of the few drivers who hate to turn it on. I never even bought one. I really don't want to hear the nastiness out there. I find the CB terribly distracting. When I was driving with Tyrone, he insisted that the CB be kept on at all times. This was a huge point of contention between us.

When I was learning to back up, it took me a lot of maneuvering around to get the truck in the slot perfectly. It was not unusual for me to spend a half hour or more at the task. What I did NOT want to hear was the jeering from a bunch of animals whose self-esteem could only be bolstered by derogatory comments about my backing ability. Listening to them, you would think that they were born knowing how to back a truck into a tight spot.

Having the CB on when you are in and around truck stops is especially disgusting. People say things that they would never say to your face, because their anonymity is insured. I have no interest in the depths of depravity of some drivers. There are separate channels on the CB that truckers use to arrange drug sales and prostitution.

Those who insist that you must have a CB radio use the argument that you need to hear about potential trouble up ahead. I counter that with, "No, I don't. If the weather is a concern, I will listen to the weather on the radio. Or I can always call the weather department at my company. They will let me know exactly what it is anywhere. As far as construction goes, I will see it when I get there. As far as cops go, I don't speed anyway, and I am glad they are there protecting us. If there is a traffic jam, that's OK. I will get off at the next suitable exit when I get into a bad jam. I will just wait it out while I prepare a meal, shower, and relax."

Another argument for the CB radio is that you must have a CB when you are at a shipper or receiver so that they can tell you when your load or your bill is ready. This is not a concern for me either. Most shippers agree to call me on my cell phone with that information. A few won't do that. So I just check back with them later and use the time to take a walk instead of waiting in my cab for a call to come over the CB. I have NEVER run into a situation where I had to have a CB.

Now you may be the opposite of me in this regard. You may love to hear gossip. You may love to chat with other drivers. You may insist that you need it to find out conditions up ahead. You may say that it is not a distraction. If so, I would say that you are in denial. ANYTHING that takes your attention away from driving is a distraction.

Tip: You don't HAVE to have a CB. I do perfectly well without one, thank you. My opinion is rare, however. Most drivers insist that it is absolutely necessary to have a CB. It's your call. Just don't think that you can't live without a CB. It's not true.

I. What if I get a ticket?

Tip: Don't get a ticket. Keep your speed down at the speed limit. The only excuse for getting a ticket is your own carelessness. Don't get distracted by talking on your phone. Always be aware of the speed limit and what is going on around you.

Tip: But if you do get a ticket, you must report it to your company ASAP. The company has to respond to the state in which you got the ticket. If the company doesn't respond right away, they will be in trouble. The minute your company finds out about a ticket that you never told them about, you will lose your job. And they WILL find out.

It is not unusual to see a driver sitting beside the road with all his packed bags looking for a ride. What happened? He got a ticket and didn't report it to the company. When they found out about it, he was fired immediately and told to leave the truck right there.

J. Avoid log violations.

Tip: Fuel first thing in the morning and log the time accurately. Fuel time is one thing that must be perfect or you will get a violation. The company computer compares the time when you pay for the fuel with the time on your logs. They must match to within 15 minutes or the computer records a violation against you.

Tip: At the end of the day, see how many miles you have driven on your odometer. Mark this at the top of your log for daily miles. Divide by 60 which is the maximum amount of miles per hour a company driver can drive without the computer giving you a violation. The number you get is the minimum number of hours you can log under driving time for the day. Do not write less driving time than this on your log. In this way you will avoid log violations.

K. How to spend more time with your spouse.

If you and your spouse like to be together all the time, perhaps you can both drive together as a team. One problem with this is that one of you is asleep while the other is driving, so you don't really spend a lot of time together.

Another option is to bring your spouse with you when you drive. This may or may not be practical depending on how much your spouse needs to work and/or wants to ride around in your truck.

You could eliminate the need for your spouse to work by getting rid of all your stuff or storing it, and living permanently in the truck. Then you wouldn't have to pay rent or a mortgage and utilities.

If your spouse wants to ride along, you will have to inform your company in advance and pay for insurance for your spouse. If you have children, you can let one (over 10 years old) at a time ride with you provided you have paid insurance for them in advance. You may only have one insured passenger at a time riding along with you.

Perhaps the best solution for you would be to find a company that will allow you to spend more time at home. I know of a company that will allow you to work a week and take a week off. But they won't hire you until you have a year's experience. Another big company will allow you to work two weeks and take a week off. But you must share trucks with other drivers. It is much easier to find a company that will let you work three weeks and take a week off. Can you be away from your spouse for three weeks at a stretch without damage to your relationship?

If you can't bear the thought of spending any time away from your loved one and you can't ride together, try to get a local job. Local jobs typically pay less than you would get with an interstate company. Local jobs typically pay you by the hour and you would get overtime. The advantage to driving locally is that you would be getting a steady paycheck without the wild fluctuations possible when driving with the big companies who drive across the country. It wouldn't hurt to check the want ads in your area before you commit to truck driving school. If there are no jobs available for a driver with no experience, and it is important to you to be home with your family, perhaps you should consider a different career.

In order to drive a dedicated route, where you will be able to go home every night, or once a week, you typically must have been employed by the company for three months with no tickets or accidents. Then, depending on the route you get, you may have to take a cut in pay.

L. Special advice for the ladies.

Ladies, by taking a few precautions, you should have no more trouble driving a truck than any of the guys out there. Truck driving may be a great opportunity for you to make a decent living doing something that you love to do.

> **Tip: Ladies, do not encourage the advances of male drivers.** You WILL see them again at the truck stop, and you do not want trouble.

When male truck drivers pull up along side me and hold up their microphones wanting me to talk, I just shrug and drive on. I have heard stories of male drivers harassing female drivers at truck stops. One very attractive woman once returned from a shower to find that her key would not unlock her truck. Some guy had put super-glue in her door lock. Then Prince Valiant came to her rescue and offered her the opportunity to sleep in his truck. The correct response to a situation like this is to immediately return to the truck stop's store, go into the ladies' room and call the police on your cell phone. Another woman told me about a man who followed her around the parking lot and then tried to crawl into her truck behind her. She kicked him in the face, knocking him back outside, and then locked her door.

Fortunately, I have not had these types of problems. Every male driver I have ever seen at a truck stop has been nothing but a gentleman. Every one of them scurries ahead and opens the door for me. I always smile and thank them.

I do carry a canister of pepper spray attached to my truck key. I also know karate and would not be afraid to use it. One of the first things I learned in karate is to stop trouble before it ever starts. If a person starts to come toward me with an unwanted advance, I would step back, put my hands out in front of me in a gesture of "stop" and give a well-practiced, blood-curdling shout of, "BACK OFF!!!!" That is usually all it would take to send him running the other way. I also avoid being out of my truck at night. I stop for the night as early as possible and park as close as possible to the rest rooms. I usually shower early in the morning and am on my way. By showering early in the morning, I avoid waiting for a shower. When I have a problem with my truck, male drivers are always eager to help me solve the problem. I am very grateful for their assistance. But they do not hit on me, because I am not giving them mixed signals. We treat each other with respect. Why do other women have problems with men when I do not? I do not dress provocatively. I wear baggy jeans and a loose T-shirt. I also wear a wedding ring. My manner of dress is that of a professional truck driver.

Tip: Ladies, what are you communicating with your dress and behavior?   When male drivers see female drivers dressed in tight jeans, halter tops, short shorts and other types of revealing clothes, they assume (rightly or wrongly) that these women would be open to their advances.

M. Looking to the future.

Now that my thirty days have passed, my leave of absence is over and I am unemployed. I have decided not to return to truck driving for some time, if ever. Although it was a fun adventure for a while, the pros no longer outweigh the cons for me. I gained a new appreciation for the difficulties and challenges faced by truck drivers. I learned to be a much more aware and safe driver. My concentration has improved. I have my CDL, which is a ticket to certain employment in a time of an uncertain economy. My health insurance enabled my husband and me to get medical care that we needed.

But I also see that I can't get my own needs met by truck driving. After spending so much time away from my husband, I no longer want to be away from him even for a single day. We have taken care of our immediate medical needs, so insurance isn't as much of an issue. It is a bit of a concern, though, and I will continue to keep my options open. At the moment, I am just one of the multitudes of uninsured Americans. I enjoyed my days driving the truck. I especially enjoyed the daily challenges of learning how to shift and back up. I enjoyed traveling all over the country when the weather was good. I enjoyed meeting new people in different parts of the country. But now it is winter and you couldn't pay me enough to go out in an 18-wheeler on windy, icy roads. I live in a part of the country where icy roads are commonplace, so taking a route in the southern part of the country wouldn't be practical for me, because I would have to drive home when I want home time, and then I would encounter difficult roads. I could always go back to driving in late spring if I feel an urgent need for health insurance. I learned a lot of lessons about how trucking companies take advantage of their students, independent contractors (lease drivers), and employees. I now see clearly how the company used me and abused me. I see that by not understanding what my choices were and by not evaluating my own needs, I allowed myself to be manipulated at every juncture by a company that has done the same thing to countless other victims and will continue to manipulate countless more.

It is my sincere hope that you will take the information in this book to heart. Keep your guard up. Stand your ground. Make logical choices that are in your own best interests. Don't be manipulated by recruiters, instructors, trainers, driver managers, and a company that is only interested in its own bottom line! Good luck!

4642499

Made in the USA
Lexington, KY
14 February 2010